T0089164

Cambridge Elements ≡

Elements in Publishing and Book Culture
edited by
Samantha Rayner
University College London
Leah Tether
University of Bristol

WHITE LITERARY TASTE PRODUCTION IN CONTEMPORARY BOOK CULTURE

Alexandra Dane
University of Melbourne

CAMBRIDGE
UNIVERSITY PRESS

CAMBRIDGE
UNIVERSITY PRESS

Shaftesbury Road, Cambridge CB2 8EA, United Kingdom

One Liberty Plaza, 20th Floor, New York, NY 10006, USA

477 Williamstown Road, Port Melbourne, VIC 3207, Australia

314–321, 3rd Floor, Plot 3, Splendor Forum, Jasola District Centre,
New Delhi – 110025, India

103 Penang Road, #05–06/07, Visioncrest Commercial, Singapore 238467

Cambridge University Press is part of Cambridge University Press & Assessment,
a department of the University of Cambridge.

We share the University's mission to contribute to society through the pursuit of
education, learning and research at the highest international levels of excellence.

www.cambridge.org
Information on this title: www.cambridge.org/9781009234245

DOI: 10.1017/9781009234276

First published 2023

A catalogue record for this publication is available from the British Library.

ISBN 978-1-009-23424-5 Paperback
ISSN 2514-8524 (online)
ISSN 2514-8516 (print)

White Literary Taste Production in Contemporary Book Culture

Elements in Publishing and Book Culture

DOI: 10.1017/9781009234276
First published online: February 2023

Alexandra Dane
University of Melbourne

Author for correspondence: Alexandra Dane, alexandra.dane@unimelb.edu.au

ABSTRACT: Despite initiatives to 'diversify' the publishing sector, there has been almost no transformation to the historic racial inequality that defines the field. This Element argues that contemporary book culture is structured by practice that operates according to a White taste logic. By applying the notion of this logic to an analysis of both traditional and new media tastemaking practices, *White Literary Taste Production in Contemporary Book Culture* examines the influence of Whiteness on the cultural practice, and how the long-standing racial inequities that characterize Anglophone book publishing are supported by systems, institutions and platforms. These themes will be explored through two distinct but interrelated case studies – women's literary prizes and anti-racist reading lists on Instagram – which demonstrate the dominance of Whiteness, and in particular White feminism, in the contemporary literary discourse.

KEYWORDS: book culture, literary tastemakers, race, Whiteness, Bourdieu

ISBNs: 9781009234245 (PB), 9781009234276 (OC)
ISSNs: 2514-8524 (online), 2514-8516 (print)

Contents

1 The Logic of White Literary Taste

In a 2021 interview with Camha Pham in *Liminal*, author and editor Radhiah Chowdhury said:

> I'll come out and say that they've [publishing houses] *always* been hostile places for FNPOC [First Nations, people of colour]writers. However much goodwill there may be for a writer of colour, this ecosystem *is not built for us*, and at some point in the life of a book, an FNPOC writer is going to come up against a wall of whiteness that will leave a mark. I guarantee it.
>
> (Chowdhury in Pham 2021, original emphasis)

This statement highlights the reality of being a First Nations person or a person of colour working in the contemporary publishing industry. Despite the often well-meaning diversity and inclusion initiatives in the publishing sector, it remains an exclusive and exclusionary site of cultural production. I am particularly struck by the image that Chowdhury conjures with the notion that the pervasive Whiteness[1] of the publishing industry will inevitably 'leave a mark', conveying both the unavoidability of working within White publishing structures in places like Australia, the United Kingdom, the United States and Canada, and the effects or impact of these structures on people of colour, and their work.

White Literary Taste Production in Contemporary Book Culture interrogates the circulation of books through contemporary culture to examine the role that Whiteness has as a foundational principle of tastemaking. This book builds the case that the Anglophone publishing sectors in Australia, the United Kingdom, Canada and the United States

---

[1] Throughout this book, I capitalise all colours that are used to describe a race (e.g. Black, White). The capitalisation of 'B' in Black has been adopted as common practice (see, for example APA Style 2022), however, I have also chosen to capitalise the 'W' in White in order to situate Whiteness as a race and challenge the historically manufactured neutrality or invisibility of Whiteness in understanding issues around race, dominance and power (Appiah 2020; National Association of Black Journalists 2020; Painter 2020).

operate according to the logic of White tastemaking where a binary assumption of who is or is not an author, and who is and is not a reader structures all practice. This is a syllogistic logic with an established structure of classification. Within this structure, an author is assumed to be White and a reader (or the audience for books) is assumed to be White. Practice within contemporary book sectors is occurring, often unconsciously, from this baseline. The existence of this logic can be seen in the pervasive and enduring inequality that defines the publishing industry in many places.

Through a study of women's literary prizes and the sharing of #AntiRacistReadingLists on social media, this book will explore the resilience of Whiteness in the publishing sector, and how this resilience perpetuates the exclusion of First Nations authors, Black authors and authors of colour from Anglophone book culture.

From some vantage points, the worldwide Black Lives Matter movement appears to have brought about a much needed and long awaited racial reckoning within the predominantly White Anglophone publishing sector. Following the murder of George Floyd in May 2020, attention to the relationship between race and the cultural industries intensified, leading to statements from majority-White institutions about #BlackLivesMatter and racial diversity within the publishing sector (Reid 2020). A week after Floyd's death, publisher Faber & Faber tweeted a thread with a list of books, starting with: 'In solidarity with the_#BlackLivesMatter movement we've pulled together a range of important books to help educate on racism and white privilege and what you can do to help enact change' (Faber Books 2020).

Faber & Faber's tweet thread is consistent with the tenor of the public communications coming from publishing houses during this time and illustrates the Anglophone publishing industry's increasing appetite for books by Black authors and authors of colour following world-wide Black Lives Matter protests. Speaking with *SBS News*, Bundjalung editor Grace Lucas-Pennington said that they:

> saw huge demand from readers and from publishers, and that's going to have a knock-on effect for the next generation of writers ... Black writing is important to me because we've always been here. We've always been telling our

stories, but they weren't getting published at the same rate as mainstream authors. (Lucas-Pennington quoted in Maunder 2021)

In addition to the promotion of books by Black authors and authors of colour, publishing houses in the United States participated in a 'day of action in solidarity with the uprisings … in response to the long history of the state-sanctioned murder of Black people' (Verso Books 2020) on 8 June 2020, and publishing houses across the globe made numerous non-specific commitments to change and to increasing 'diversity' (Viltus 2020). These statements about change and tweets about resources for interrogating structural racism do represent a shift in the ways that the publishing sector has traditionally approached issues of race and diversity. While there were some well-publicised appointments of Black women into high-profile roles in major conglomerate publishing houses (Reid 2020), beyond this there appears to have been little meaningful systemic change in the industry.

The issues that define Black Lives Matter protests within the publishing sector have, as Chowdhury (2021) observes, always existed. In her 1992 monograph, *Playing in the Dark: Whiteness and Literary Imagination*, Toni Morrison explores the relationship between American literary criticism, literary reception and race. In articulating the foundational principles of the American literary field, Morrison uncovers the ways in which these principles and the structures they uphold intersect with the critical reception of literary texts. Morrison writes:

> I have been thinking about the validity or vulnerability of a certain set of assumptions conventionally accepted among literary historians and critics and circulated as 'knowledge'. This knowledge holds that traditional, canonical American literature is free of, uninformed, and unshaped by the four-hundred-year-old presence of, first, Africans and then African-Americans in the United States. It assumes that this presence – which shaped the body politic, the Constitution, and the entire history of the culture – has had no significant place or consequence in the origin and development of that culture's literature. (Morrison 1992, 4)

In the thirty years since *Playing in the Dark* was published, there has been little change in the relationship between race and the literary field, or any revision to the assumptions around knowledge production, race and cultural circulation that Morrison (1992) describes. The 2020 Black Lives Matter protests are perhaps one of the first times that major publishing houses and cultural intermediaries have, across the board, publicly grappled with the role that racism plays in perceptions and assumptions around authority, knowledge production and notions of legitimacy. Richard Jean So calls this 'cultural redlining', a practice that results in a cultural field wherein 'white authors exercise a distinct racial command over minority authors, particularly Black novelists' (So 2021, 3). So notes that 'Cultural redlining, much like economic redlining, does not happen at the level of the individual writer, page or text. It happens at a cognitive scale well beyond what a single person can observe or read' (So 2021, 6). What So is describing here is the overwhelming force of Whiteness, a logic that structures activities in book culture, influencing production, circulation and reception.

Echoing Morrison's articulation of cultural industry assumptions, the prevailing theme that runs through Anamik Saha and Sandra van Lente's 'Re:Thinking "Diversity" in Publishing' (2020) report is the notion that publishing professionals have well-developed assumptions around who reads books and who should be writing them. The report's findings, which emerge from interviews with 113 publishing industry professionals, demonstrate how the industry works to serve a 'core audience' of White, middle-class readers, and how questions around the perceived 'quality' of authors of colour pervade conversations around acquisitions. This is the logic of White taste: who is/is not an author, who is/is not a reader. When conversations around acquisitions and authors of colour are tied to questions of quality, the assumption within the logic of White taste that authors are White is reinforced. Similarly, if the primary audience for books is assumed to be White, books *for* White audiences is the core business.[2]

---

[2] For a detailed discussion of the role of 'comps' and the ways in which this acquisition practice perpetuates the Whiteness of the industry, see McGrath (2019).

These two findings, among others, illustrate the rigidity of White supremacy in the contemporary publishing sector, and the difficulties of transforming systems rooted in racist ideals. We can see this theme echoed in Radhiah Chowdhury's report into diversity in the Australian publishing sector. Chowdhury (2021) writes, 'Assumptions of audience are why any attempts to make mainstream publishing more inclusive cannot solely rely on a handful of diversity initiatives or focus on one aspect of the publishing foodchain.' I linger here on these assumptions around audiences and authors that Chowdhury and Saha and van Lente identify because it is these assumptions – and the network of associated perceptions that stem from and intersect with them – that are the focus of this book.

In this book, I interrogate the role that the logic of White taste plays in contemporary book culture. So (2021, 14) contends that 'Whiteness constitutes a driving force in the articulation of canonical American fiction'. Extending this idea, I contend that more than a driving force, Whiteness is a defining feature of publishing practice in many Anglophone contemporary publishing industries, particularly in the United Kingdom, the United States, Australia and Canada and informs a logic against which activity is performed.

There is a strong corpus of contemporary research that examines the effects of Whiteness in contemporary publishing (see, for example, Melanie Ramdarshan Bold's (2019) work into young adult fiction and authors of colour; Anamik Saha and Sandra van Lente's (2022) work into diversity efforts and their effects and, Richard Jean So's (2021) research on race and the American canon), research that demonstrates the ways in which authors and readers of colour are consistently sidelined and marginalised by the industry and those who work within its confines. The contribution that this book makes to this field of research is an examination of not only the dominance of White individuals within the industry but also the dominance of Whiteness as the logic that informs cultural tastes in book culture. Coming from the perspective of the circulation of book *culture* – as opposed to the production of books themselves – I seek to identify and analyse this logic in practice. In exploring the notion of a White logic of literary taste production, the ontology of logic is difficult to avoid. At their most basic, the laws of non-contradiction, of identity and of the excluded middle (Olson 2007, 551) tell us a lot about the ways in which a logic of White taste production might operate within the contemporary publishing sector: all things can be classified as either inside or outside of a group leaving little room for nuance or intersectionality. The logic of White taste primarily classifies an author as White and a reader as White. Author and readers who fall outside this classification are understood to be nested in a sub-classification: a Black author, a reader of colour. Moreover, the ubiquity of this logic in both the systems that organise information and traditional scholarly pursuits means that it is embedded into the fabric of publishing and contemporary book culture.

Efforts towards Diversity

Progress towards change can often be perceived as linear, a perception that assumes, for example, representation for racial minorities within spaces dominated by White people is stronger today than it was a decade ago. This assumption around the nature of progress is misguided and reveals a perception of the inertia of progress that does not exist. For example, sporadic interventions into the publishing industry aimed at establishing greater equality for women authors have brought about meaningful but short-lived gains, establishing a picture of progress that is defined by peaks and troughs as opposed to sustained growth (Dane 2020c, 83). Research into the representation of authors of colour in the British publishing sector reveals that there were more authors of colour published in Britain in 2006 than there were in 2016 (Ramdarshan Bold 2019, 107). Ramdarshan Bold's work suggests that regression might have occurred because from the early-2000s, 'publishers now had a small pool of established authors of colour to draw from', and were not working to nurture and develop new authors of colour beyond this core group (Ramdarshan Bold 2019, 107). This phenomenon is echoed in So's study of the US publishing sector, where he describes the ways in which individual authors of colour 'join the ranks' of the literary elite, to the exclusion of others: 'when literary gatekeepers admit Black authors into the literary 1 percent, they do so with very specific rules of inclusion. They will only distribute their attention in highly unequal terms' (2021, 82). We see through these two examples that progress towards equality is non-linear because of the ways in which the 'literary elite' or 'gatekeepers' work to retain the power of the dominant group. The inertia at play within this cultural sector is not towards equality, rather, towards inequality. This, in turn, raises questions around the role that efforts to bring about equality, or at least increase diversity play in today's publishing sector.

It is worth examining the attempts individuals and organisations have made to establish equality in the publishing sector, and explore why these attempts often do not bring about the systemic change they seek. Statements around diversity and inclusion are a common presence on the websites of multinational publishing houses, many offering a commitment to increasing the diversity of the publishing workforce. For example, Penguin Random House US's (2021) 'Diversity, Equity & Inclusion' webpage details the myriad initiatives the company supports in order to transform the entrenched inequalities of their company and the industry more broadly. The site states:

> Establishing more inclusive business practices – including reflecting the diversity of our world in our staff – is a necessity for us to help build an inclusive society. For us, more diverse publishing is not just a moral imperative … We will increase the number of books we publish – and promote, market, and sell – by people of color. (Penguin Random House 2021)

Hachette UK adopts a similar, albeit more specific, approach to equality and diversity in their organisation, saying: 'We have been voluntarily publishing our ethnicity pay gap since 2019 and pledged a representation target of 15% of the total group workforce for Black, Asian and Minority Ethnic talent within five years' (Hachette 2021). What is clear from these two examples is that publishing houses are cognisant of the fact that, for example, 87 per cent of the UK's publishing workforce is White (Publishers Association 2020), a statistic that is replicated in other national contexts (Chowdhury 2021). What is unclear from these statements is the role that the logic of White taste plays in both the industry's glaring inequalities and in the ways in which equality will be brought about. I argue that this omission serves a purpose.

In their research examining the limitations and the realities of diversity efforts in book production and contemporary publishing, Anamik Saha and Sandra van Lente (2022, 1808, 1813, 1815) observe the ways in which efforts to establish a more inclusive or diverse publishing industry in the United Kingdom consistently fail to achieve their aims. They write, 'Diversity is effectively mobilised on the terms of Whiteness, which simultaneously commodifies and marginalises narratives around race' (Saha and Lente 2022, 1806). Saha and van Lente go on to note that, 'this is a central feature of the publishing industry, which operates to sustain privilege as much as to make profit' (2022, 1806) complicating the industry-wide assumptions around the power of diversity and inclusion efforts to bring about meaningful change. This complication targets not simply the diversity and inclusion efforts themselves but interrogates how these initiatives: obscure the root cause of inequality; uphold Whiteness as the dominant standard against which diversity is understood; and, render equality as a commodity. Saha and van Lente's research shows how publishers, throughout the publishing process, continually reinforce the dominance of Whiteness. Thinking about this in the context of Penguin Random House's (2021) statement on diversity and inclusion, I argue that the conglomerate publisher seeks to establish more inclusive business practices and commits to publishing more authors of colour, under the assumption that these acts will bring about the 'inclusive society' they seek to promote. This statement positions the publishing house itself as the benevolent White force to bring about change, without even entertaining the possibility that this dominance could be or should be challenged.

This White dominance influences all facets of book culture and is rooted in established ideas about legitimacy and authority. There exists a relationship between the notions of what constitutes legitimacy and the influence of Whiteness in the production of literary tastes. The cultural engagement among the most dominant groups within a society comes to define the notions of legitimate culture and legitimate cultural production (Bourdieu 1984, 280). Understood in the context of 'race making' that Saha and van Lente put forward helps us to see the complex and interactive system of Whiteness that underpins activities within publishing and contemporary book culture, and the ways in which this system works to be and remain self-fulfilling.

Whiteness and the Acquisitions Process

Perhaps the clearest articulation of this system of dominance comes from the process of acquisitions in the publishing industry. The acquisition process is one that is cloaked in mystery and mythos, where proclamations around taste, 'gut feeling' and industry nous are foregrounded (Squires 2017). The process of 'getting published' – and the relationship between this process and race – is one that is examined in great depth by both Ramdarshan Bold (2019) and by Saha (2016). Ramdarshan Bold's research highlights how publishers and editors (a group of professionals that are overwhelmingly White (Publishers Association 2020)) appear to consistently limit the kinds of books they publish from authors of colour. Despite apparent increasing demand for books written by authors of colour (Maunder 2021) this research indicates that authors of colour are expected to write about 'issues' that relate to race or conform to a particular stereotype or narrative (Ramdarshan Bold 2019, 114–15). It appears that the individuals who are commissioning new works of fiction and non-fiction lack the imagination to perceive that authors of colour could or should write beyond a particular type of story. Whether this limited imagination is consciously or sub-consciously performed, it reveals the prevalence of a White taste logic that forms the foundation of decision-making. The development of point-of-sales technology that has facilitated a rise in 'data-driven' acquisition decisions has only worked to reinforce this logic (Saha 2016, 4). When the opportunities for authors are limited by the racialised imagination, and therefore acquisitions decisions, of publishers (Ramdarshan Bold 2019), the input data for point-of-sales software will result in sales data that ultimately supports these assumptions.

The way that perceptions of Whiteness, authority and legitimacy pervade acquisition decision-making processes, and the strength of this logic in the contemporary publishing sector, plays out in ways that are counterproductive to the economic imperatives and profit motives of commercial trade publishing. The industry-wide assumptions around who reads books and who is best placed to write them, assumptions that work to support the dominance of White individuals and White structures in the publishing sector, place limitations on the potential profitability of books. Saha writes, 'if capitalism were only concerned with profit, then it would be in the best interests of sales and marketing to stress the universal qualities of the cultural commodity rather than brand it according to race' (Saha 2016, 11). This contradiction highlights the strength of the logic of White tastemaking and the ability for the logic to influence practices in a way that undermines a profit motive.

I take Saha and van Lente's work into the 'race making' of the contemporary publishing sector as the foundation for this study into the notion of Whiteness and taste in book culture. Rather than focus on the production side of the publishing industry, my work largely examines the culture that surrounds a book post-publication and the ways in which Whiteness underpins taste production. Through this examination, I demonstrate the rigidity of White literary taste production and how this tastemaking force reverberates through the industry. Through two case studies – women's literary prizes and anti-racist reading lists shared on social media – I contend that the logic of White taste operates in both conscious and sub-conscious ways to continually establish and re-establish White dominance in book publishing and book culture.

Structure of the Book

Interrogating the logic of White taste in this volume starts in Chapter 2 'Legitimacy, Value and Power' with an exploration of the foundational principles that inform the structures of contemporary book culture. In this chapter I examine the principles upon which the contemporary publishing sector and the logic of White taste was established, and test this logic within the sub-fields of book criticism, and online and offline sales. In this chapter I offer the notion of practice–structure–practice (Bourdieu 1977) as the foundation for understanding the ever-perpetuating assumptions around what constitutes an author and bring these ideas into play with critical Whiteness studies. This chapter establishes the theoretical context for the two case studies that form Chapters 3 and 4.

In Chapter 3, 'The Whiteness of Women's Literary Awards', I explore the ways in which women's literary prizes in the United Kingdom and in Australia perpetuate the dominance of White authors within and beyond these two literary markets. I examine the literary prize and the popular discourse that surrounds the prize as a process of myth-making and the way that White feminist solipsism works to further both the myths that structure prize discourse and the racial inequality that lies at their core. This chapter interrogates the operation of the White taste logic beyond publishing practice and into broader book culture, a theme that continues into Chapter 4.

Chapter 4, 'The Transformative Limits of the Anti-Racist Reading List', looks at the ways that the logic of White taste intersects with the Black Lives Matter movement and the notion of 'doing the work'. This chapter interrogates the reader as a contemporary literary tastemaker, the perceived value of reading, and the role of cultural capital in both book culture and in social media discourse. This chapter examines the adoption of 'giving a voice' or 'amplifying voices' rhetoric by White readers in book culture, and tests whether the popularity of anti-racist reading lists on Twitter and Instagram can influence bestseller lists and challenge the dominance of White authors.

2 Legitimacy, Value and Power

The racial inequality that defines contemporary Anglophone book culture is part of a broader socially supported structure of Whiteness. However, focusing on the publishing sector and the production, circulation and reception of books is not simply an examination of the *effects* of White supremacist societal structures. Book publishing, and the associated discourses that constitute book culture, is a cultural sector that is actively involved in knowledge production and circulation, and a cultural sector that defines and redefines notions of authority and creative and intellectual legitimacy (Dane 2020c, 204). In this way, the inequality that characterises book publishing is not simply a by-product of broader racist societal structures, book publishing is an active participant in maintaining the rigidity of these structures. Writing in *The Atlantic* about the radiating effects of inequities in YA publishing, Jen Doll (2012) notes that 'books transmit values, and if you don't find yourself in books … you have to reach the conclusion that you are less valuable'. This chapter explores the foundation, context and affects of the logic of White taste, and looks to book reviewing, online bookselling and bestseller lists to demonstrate the logic in action.

David Hesmondhalgh and Anamik Saha's (2013) research into the relationship between race and cultural production echoes Doll's assertion in their exploration of how White racist structures and ontologies circulate within and then move beyond the cultural industry. In doing so, Hesmondhalgh and Saha (2013, 183) observe the ways in which:

> The effects of racism and the racialization of ethnicity permeate institutions of cultural production, and, because such production significantly shapes the knowledge, values and benefits that are circulated in society, the continuing influence in cultural production is likely to have effects on societies.

In the introduction, I touched on the diversity initiatives that conglomerate publishers introduced in the wake of the global Black Lives Matter protests in 2020. Saha and van Lente's (2022) research interrogates how efforts like these are not only unlikely to realise the change they seek, but are also a representation of the racialized structures of the industry at work. This idea is a foundational principle for this book, raising questions about not just publishing houses and book production practices, but also the ways in which these practices and the structures that underpin them ripple out into the broader culture (Ahmed 2012, 21, 34). In an examination of the precarity of diversity efforts in the creative industries, Herman Gray (2016, 246) questions:

> Whether correctives to inequality can be addressed by the exchange of bodies and experiences responsible for making content, rather than by exposing the assumptions, micro-practices, social relations and power dynamics that define our collective cultural common sense about the nature of social difference and the practices of inequality.

Here, Gray exposes the disconnect between broad-based diversity efforts that aim to address the composition of workplaces and, in the case of the publishing sector, the composition of authors on lists and the myriad assumptions and 'micropractices' that are not simply the roots of the representation inequality but also the reasons why the inertia of inequality remains. These assumptions and micropractices are rooted in the logic of White taste, a syllogistic logic that prescribes what is/is not an author, and what is/is not a reader.

In interrogating the way that this logic influences production, circulation and reception in book culture, it is helpful to examine the relationship between structure and practice. Bourdieu's articulation of a theory of practice (1977) reveals the interconnected and symbiotic ties between structure and practice in the field of cultural production, the two existing in an infinitely and continuously generative relationship (Bourdieu 1993). What defines the nature of this relationship is the habitus, that is, the disposition or 'conditions of existence' (Bourdieu 1977, 72) of both the field and of those who operate within its structure. Agents within the field of cultural production, in this case the book publishing sector, have a habitus that is informed by their socio-cultural environment and interactions. This habitus is built upon practice and interaction, which in turn informs practice and interaction. In this way, the present structural environmental or collective habitus or disposition is structured by past practice, and the future habitus is structured by the present. However, it does offer the opportunity for transformation. With changes to structures, and not simply personnel, practice can follow.

Bourdieu (1977, 85) observes that 'the habitus is the product of the work of inculcation and appropriation necessary in order for those products of collective history, and the objective structures ... to succeed in reproducing themselves more or less completely'. The interconnected and generative nature of structure and practice is helpful for understanding the perpetuation of a particular structural disposition: this is the coming together of an invisible sociocultural consensus. However, it is also important to consider the values that underpin this disposition, why it takes a particular form and the reasons for its durability. Bourdieu calls these values the doxa: the 'schemes of thought and perception' that underpin the collective habitus of a field, producing in individuals a sense of objectivity or truth based on subjectivities (Bourdieu 1977, 164).

> The instruments of knowledge of the social world are in this case (objectively) political instruments which contribute to the reproduction of the social world by producing immediate adherence to the world, seen as self-evident and undisputed, of which they are the product and of which they reproduce the structure in a transformed form. (Bourdieu 1977, 164)

The logic of White taste is a major component of the doxa of book culture. This logic is the subjective structure of classification built upon racially-informed assumptions. It is a structure that through practice – publishing, reviewing, awarding, discussing – is supported and reproduced again and again. The doxa remains unexamined and uninterrogated because it is constructed to appear self-evident, 'history turned into nature' (Bourdieu 1977, 78). Bourdieu regards this structured and self-generating practice as the operation of a 'conductorless orchestra' (85), invoking the sense that the collective habitus keeps a given field or social structure balanced and in harmony. The image of a conductorless orchestra illustrates the invisibility of the self-perpetuating relationship between structure and practice, however, in doing so, it blurs the significant influence of practice. The orchestra is not conductorless, rather, the conductor is often invisible to us. The conductor's sense of harmony is built upon prior understandings of balance. These prior understandings continue to inform, perhaps subconsciously, a projected definition of author identity.

The Author and the Authority to Write

Authors are the most visible and recognisable individuals in book publishing and broader book culture. This visibility is not a contemporary phenomenon, however, the prominence of individual authors within book culture has grown throughout the twentieth and twenty-first centuries (Driscoll 2014; Weber 2018). In pondering the definition of 'the author', Foucault (1969) argues that the name of an author can – and often does – sit outside of and separate to the texts they have created (304). In this way, the author exists not just as a signifier but as the signified. Writing about the emerging literary culture of the nineteenth century, Foucault (1969, 306) notes that, '"Literary" discourse was acceptable only if it carried an author's name ... the meaning and value attributed to the text depended on this information'. Here we can begin to see how the name and profile of the author have long been integral to the public circulation and reception of their work. Foucault goes on to describe the relational exchange between the literary culture and the definition of the author, noting that:

> This construction is assigned a 'realistic' dimension as we speak of an individual's 'profundity' or 'creative' power, his intentions or the original inspiration manifested in writing ... These aspects of an individual, which we designate as an author (or which comprise an individual as an author), are projections, in terms always more or less psychological, of our ways of handling texts. (1969, 307)

Interrogating Foucault's articulation of what an author is and what an author means reveals many of the assumptions around authors and notions of authority that inform White taste logic and continue to structure contemporary book culture (Chowdhury 2021; Saha and van Lente 2022). While Foucault's articulation of the way that the author is constructed does not explicitly examine the relationship between this construction and race, it does raise questions around whose projections are being placed on the manifested definition of the author and their place in book culture. This idea of projection is reminiscent of Bourdieu's examination of the struggle for the power to define legitimacy within the field of cultural production wherein the dominant class maintains their dominance by defining and redefining legitimacy in their image (Bourdieu 1977).

If the prevailing definition of an author is constructed around racist assumptions of who is and is not an author, it follows that notions of authority and legitimacy that structure contemporary book culture are working within a racialised logic. As Ramdarshan Bold (2019, 97) notes, 'Authors of colour challenge the perception of what … British literature is. Canonical authors, commonly white, middle class and male, usually have the monopoly on defining Britishness in the literature.' Ramdarshan Bold's observation illustrates the ways in which dominant perceptions and assumptions around authority within the literary field both circulate within and permeate the bounds of book culture. This is reminiscent of Morrison's (1992, 9) questioning of the relationship between Whiteness and the American literary imaginary: 'What parts do the invention and development of whiteness play in the construction of what is loosely described as "American"?' Ramdarshan Bold's and Morrison's articulation of the inextricable relationship between White canonical authors and the definition of British or American literature is reflected in another national context in the criteria of the Miles Franklin Literary Award (Australia's most prestigious literary prize), which is awarded to 'the novel of the year which is of the highest literary merit and which must present Australian life in any of its phases' (Allington 2011). How might the Australian literary field understand 'Australianness', and how does race intersect with this definition of 'Australian life', in the context of national literary consecration?

The 'Australian life in any of its phases' criterion that structures the process of judging the Miles Franklin Literary Award has been the topic of annual discussion in the cultural pages of national newspapers and throughout book culture since the 1950s. Much of this discussion centres around the issue of the eligibility (or ineligibility) of particular titles, and what it means to write about Australian life. Since the prize was first awarded in 1957, a number of titles have been excluded from consideration because they were not set in Australia, and did not have Australian characters or an Australian protagonist (Allington 2011). The, perhaps unintended, consequence of the inclusion of this criterion and the ways that judging panels have adopted varying degrees of faithfulness to its interpretation is that the overwhelming majority of novels that have won the Miles Franklin Literary Award are historical, set in rural and remote places, and focus on White male settler narratives: 'Blokes, the past, the bush', as Lamond (2011) observed. In exploring the limitations of the 'Australian life' criterion, Brian Castro notes that '"Australia in any of its phases" is ambiguous in that the emphasis is on canon-making ahead of complexity' (quoted in Allington 2011). Castro's observation, of 'canon-making ahead of complexity', speaks not only of the difficulties of adjudicating both the best novel of the year that is also the novel that portrays Australian life, but also of the ways in which canon formation is an act of nationalism that, in the Australian context, prioritises White settler stories. Since 1957, there have been sixty-four winners of the Miles Franklin Literary Award. Fifty-seven (or 89 per cent) of the winners were White, and seven (11 per cent) were First Nations authors or authors of colour. Up until 2000, every single winner of the Miles Franklin Literary Award was White. Thinking about these figures against the backdrop of Castro's observation about nationalism and canon formation we can begin to see the way that the White taste logic intersects with imaginary literary canons, and flows out beyond the prize and the discussion of canons into book culture.

To understand the blanket dominance of White authors and publishers and critics and judges in Anglophone book culture, we need to examine the sector from above to see all the moving and immobile parts. bell hooks' work provides a structure for understanding the interconnected cycle of authority, whiteness, the publishing industry and taste that I seek to explore in this book. hooks' ideas on writing, literature and Black culture (1989, 2012) are similarly explored in Morrison's (1992), Ramdarshan Bold's (2019) and Saha and Van Lente's (2022) examinations of racialised particularities of authority and legitimacy. hooks draws a line between the publishing industry's idealised author, the assumed authority of this idealised figure, and the academy, highlighting the ways in which this interconnection is established in universities and reinforced throughout wider book culture (1989, 42, 43). For hooks, the roots of the assumptions and perceptions of authority are in the subject/object dichotomy that has long structured the practice of White people researching and writing *about* Black people and people of colour. On this practice, hooks (1989, 42) notes that 'As objects, one's reality is defined by others, one's identity is created by others, one's history is named only in ways that define one's relationship to those who are subject.' In establishing a binary definition around the assumed identity of 'the author', the logic of White taste creates objects out of those who fall outside this definition, the 'not author' side of the logical equation. The projected authority of White authors writing about Black people can only exist within a system where Black voices are made absent or are dismissed as lacking an authorial legitimacy that is defined and maintained by the dominant group. In this way, we can start to see not simply the ways that book culture and the publishing industry are situated within and feed into broader cultural and intellectual structures, but also how this culture is a product of notions of authority and the subject, born in the academy. The authority of the White author within this structure is dependent on the absence – the manufactured absence – of Black authors and authors of colour.

Sketching out this interconnected relationship of perceived authority, manufactured legitimacy and race illustrates the systemic nature of the dominance of White literary taste in book culture. hooks invokes the notion of White supremacy (over, for example, racism) to interrogate structures of legitimacy in both the academy and in the literary culture, as it more accurately describes not only the systemic but also the pervasive nature of the structures that maintain the dominance of White people (authors, editors, publishers) in the sector. Moreover, by examining White supremacy and White supremacist practices, hooks encourages us to look beyond the 'overtly racist discrimination, exploitation and oppression of Black people', and to focus our attention on the 'ideology that most determines how White people ... irrespective of their political leanings to the left or right ... relate to Black people and people of colour' (1989, 113). Shifting our gaze from explicit and individualised racist actions towards a more opaque ideology is useful for trying to understand the pervasiveness and dominance of White tastemaking in book culture as it allows us to interrogate the ways in which White liberal or left-leaning individuals operate within, perpetuate, and affirm a system of racial domination and oppression (hooks 1989, 113). Analysing the radiating influence of White tastemaking as a structural logic – as opposed to individualised, piecemeal acts designed to oppress other individuals – brings to light not only the continued dominance of this structure but also the ways in which the influence of structured White tastemaking can be obfuscated and misrecognised by the White liberals who are so strongly represented in book culture.

The contemporary Anglophone publishing industry can be characterised as one where White, left/progressive-identifying, middle-class and tertiary-educated people are in the vast majority. Contemporary research illustrates the self-image that many individuals working in the publishing sector possess, and the ways in which this self-image intersects with the realities of race and publishing practice (Saha 2016, 2). I would argue that many White people working in contemporary Anglophone book culture would classify them-selves as critical-thinking progressives working towards a more diverse and inclusive cultural sector. However, much of the work designed to bring about a more diverse sector is focused on individual action and not systemic change (Ahmed 2012; Saha and van Lente 2022). hooks (1989, 114) observes the 'pressures to assimilate' that Black people experiences when they enter social contexts that continue to operate with White supremacist logics, assimilation that may help to meet 'diversity' targets but which does little to dismantle or challenge the foundational structure. The strength of this individualised system is reinforced by the individualised 'assimilation' that hooks describes and, in the case of the publishing sector, flows beyond the production and into the circulation and reception of books.

hooks' observation anticipates So's (2021, 79) exploration of cultural redlining, where So illustrates the outcomes of the 'Toni Morrison effect' – simply put, a phenomenon wherein the White dominant book culture 'admits' one Black author or author of colour into the imagined literary canon to, in part, demonstrate racial inclusion or progressive ideals – a practice that validates the logic of the status quo among White liberals. What is perhaps the clearest articulation of the structure of White supre-macy that is so integral to contemporary Anglophone book culture is both the invisibility of this structure in operation among many working in book culture – publishers, editors, critics, administrators – together with the very visible outcomes that this structure produces, for example, the stark racial inequality of literary prize shortlists or the paucity of Black authors and authors of colour within the book review pages of major cultural publications (So 2021, 98). hooks writes of assumed annual 'publishing quotas' for fiction written by Black women, noting that 'such quotas are not consciously negotiated and decided upon but are the outcomes of institutionalised racism, sexism and classism' (1989, 143). I argue that the 'quotas' that hooks observes are part of the inertia of Whiteness in book culture that works to keep the structure of White dominance in place. The foundation of this inertia is the White taste logic that is formed around assumptions around legitimacy and value of writing by Black authors and authors of colour, and the ways in which these assumptions flow beyond systems of book production to become influential but often invisible markers of taste within book culture.

Whiteness and Book Reviewing

Examining the cultural sub-field of literary criticism and book reviewing is useful for illustrating how literary consensus, built on the long-standing and deeply entrenched White taste logic, can be continually perpetuated and reinforced through cultural practice. Central to the continued survival of this logic is a competitive hierarchy of power where the dominant are afforded the privilege of establishing the boundaries of consensus (van Rees 1987). However, it is not just artists or authors who jostle for dominant positions. By participating in the cultural field, *all* actors involved in cultural production – critics, reviewers, editors, publishers – are involved in the competition for definitional authority (Bourdieu 1993). The principles and values that underpin a cultural field like the publishing sector are rooted in broader socio-structural values and, at the same time, the activity of the field and the structure of field hierarchies ensure that these principles are maintained. The practice of reviewing a book emerges from, and exists in relation to, a field-wide understanding of the definition of 'literature'. In reviewing a book, the reviewer feeds back into the parameters of this definition and establishes a link between the author and their book, and this definition. Texts and authors who attract significant critical attention, particularly in cases when broad consensus among critics and reviewers is reached, influence the field's foundational definition of literature, as do the established critics and reviewers that form the consensus around a text/ author (van Rees 1987, 280, 284). The work of critics and reviewers is not so much an act of the assessment of value against the consensus definition, but is more akin to a process of assigning value in accordance with the consensus definition.

Author reputations are built and maintained, in part, through continual and sustained critical attention. This perpetual interaction occurs within the structure of a logic that relies on the long-standing assumptions about authorial legitimacy and a projected idea of the reading public. In their study of cultural consecration, Cattani et al. (2014, 275) highlight the interest that the dominant actors in a social and cultural field have in structural 'continuity', and how the limited consecratory opportunities for those on the periphery of the field are often attained only by those who 'share the same or similar dispositions' (276) to the dominant actors. Cattani et al. (2014) description of the field of cultural production calls back to Bourdieu's (1993) articulation of the field and how it operates according to a logic that maintains a White-dominant status quo. The zero-sum consensus around books that are considered 'good' (worthy of attention) or 'not good' (not worthy of attention) is shaped in part by forces beyond the aesthetic properties of a text. The effects of the underlying logic of White taste production in book criticism can be seen in the history of book reviewing in the United States wherein White authors have consistently constituted around 90 per cent of the most reviewed authors each year between 1965 and 2000 (So 2021, 70).

I would argue that there are two interrelated factors that underpin this dominance. The first factor is the inclusion/exclusion binary that is inherent in the process of book reviewing. If sustained critical attention is an essential element in an author's literary reputation, 'each moment of attention' So writes, 'marks a moment of inclusion, yet at the same time it also marks a moment of exclusion' (2021, 78). Thinking back on the notion of the 'assumed' publishing quota for Black women that hooks describes

(1989, 143), we can see that when critical attention is finite and inclusion for one author means exclusion for another, the interest in structural continuity for those in dominant positions follows the logic of White taste. The second factor is rooted in the constructed notions of authorial legitimacy. Taking Foucault's (1969) and Ramdarshan Bold's (2019) interrogations of the identity of an author according to the cultural imaginary, the reasons for the historic and continued dominance of White authors in contemporary book reviewing – as both authors reviewed and as reviewers (Dane 2020c, 199) – are pulled into focus. So's study observes the ways in which reviewers in America's most culturally important magazines, newspapers and periodicals engage with a broad range of writing by White authors but review only a narrow selection of writing by Black authors. He writes:

> When reviewers look at novels by white authors, they tend to look at a broad range of white authors. But when they look at novels by black authors, they tend to look at only a very, very few … The valorization of a single black author in the field means that a number of less distinguished black authors get pushed to the margins of attention. (So 2021, 82–3)

The continuing practice of book reviewing affords White authors not only more opportunities to attract critical attention but more power to define and influence the parameters of literary understanding. In this way, Black authors not only are 'pushed to the margins' in terms of the critical attention and promotional opportunities that reviewing brings but also are 'pushed to the margins' of the cultural imagination of the assumed identity of an author.

Critical Whiteness Studies

Critical Whiteness studies, as a branch of critical race theory, provides a helpful framework for interrogating the role and influence of Whiteness in the production, reproduction and dominance of White taste in book culture. The essential role of invisibility in the ongoing relationship between Whiteness and power was observed and explored by W. E. B DuBois (1935), and has formed the foundation of much of the research into

Whiteness and power that has followed. By exploring practices in contemporary book culture through the lens of critical Whiteness studies, the White supremacist structures that hooks (1989, 2012) and So (2021) describe – that are, by design, invisible – are pulled into focus. The aim of critical Whiteness studies is to interrogate locations of power and privilege, explore the ways in which this location is inextricably linked with race, and elucidate how the dominance of Whiteness is maintained by a constructed invisibility and the notion that the dominant group is 'both the norm and the ideal of what it means to be human' (Steyn and Conway 2010, 284). The notion of the invisibility of Whiteness within a cultural context or system of power is central to critical Whiteness studies and is a theme that runs through the significant research into race and cultural production explored in this book (see, for example, hooks 1989; Morrison 1992, 9; Hesmondhalgh and Saha 2013, 183; Saha 2016, 5). Considering the field of cultural production through this theoretical lens illuminates the role of race as an integral element in the maintenance of the field's hierarchy of power.

Taking the constructed and deliberate invisibility of Whiteness as the starting point for the exploration of the influence and dominance of a White taste logic in contemporary book culture facilitates an exploration that moves beyond individuals and individualised practices and allows us to see the interconnected systems of power that book culture is both situated within and helps to maintain. Central to the continued dominance of Whiteness and White tastes in book culture is the cultural practices that are institutionally sanctioned and, therefore, reproduced and reinforced (Twine and Gallagher 2008, 6, 13). Approaching the study of Whiteness and book culture as both a system and as a practice ensures that our analysis is taken beyond the 'White body' and the practices of White individuals, avoiding both the traps of racial essentialism and individualism (Nayak 2007, 743). In an examination of the intersection of race and Bourdieu's articulation of cultural capital, Derron Wallace (2018) observes how the markers of cultural capital that are often attributed by scholars to White individuals reinforce the relationship between Whiteness and elevated cultural capital. Wallace's research is helpful in the context of this book because it not only illustrates how notions of cultural capital are established by the reproduction of particular knowledges and cultural tastes but also how researchers who interrogate the ethno-racial nature of cultural capital consistently highlight the White middle-classes as the group with the cultural touchpoints that Bourdieu describes (468). In doing so, researchers 'fortify perceptions of Whiteness as an intrinsic feature of cultural capital' (Wallace 2018, 468). Wallace's work illustrates how White structures play out and are supported on multiple levels. It is useful to again briefly linger on Bourdieu and his articulation of the interconnected nature of cultural tastes, cultural capital and symbolic capital (1984, 228), and how we can understand this relationship against the backdrop of critical Whiteness studies.

Bourdieu (1984) explores the ways in which taste production, and reproduction, is rooted in the struggle for power/authority/legitimacy among the individual cultural producers and actors within a given field. Changing cultural tastes, Bourdieu contends, will result in corresponding transformations in the structure and dispositions of a cultural field, and the dominant actors within a given cultural field will possess not only the authority to define the parameters of legitimate cultural production but also the parameters of legitimate cultural taste. Moreover, Bourdieu (1984, 323) describes the 'pre-established harmony' of interests between those who are involved with the production and dissemination of 'legitimate culture' and those who seek to both consume and inhabit proximity to 'legitimate culture', assumptions around these two groups form the foundation of the logic of White taste. Here we can conceptualise the practice of taste production and influence of individuals within a cultural field, however, Bourdieu's attachment to the notion of a struggle for positions within the field trains our attentions to the actions and practices of – and between – individuals, and away from the ways that individual cultural practice exists within and is shaped by broader structural forces that are, in turn, upheld and perpetuated by cultural practice. The issues that Wallace (2018, 468) raises with empirical engagements with Bourdieu's work highlight the limits of Bourdieu's notions of cultural power and cultural taste production, as well as the limited ways in which scholars have applied these ideas to various contexts. It is important for scholars appropriating Bourdieu in examinations of race and power to not sever the ties between individual action and structural forces. In doing so, we risk placing the power of transformation with individual action, obfuscating the influence of the logics of cultural taste.

Information Logics as Taste Logics

The discipline of information systems and knowledge organisation can offer us insights into the explicit relationship between logic or deductive reasoning and the structured distribution of symbolic and economic capital in the field. Amazon's classification structures and practices, and the ways that these structures and practices uphold the dominance of White authors on the platform, is a contemporary illustration of the effects of both long-standing approaches to knowledge organisation and how, in establishing the terms or parameters upon which knowledge organisation is based, the dominant group encode both their dominance and the invisibility of this dominance.

There is a strong relationship between the logics that underpin legacy information systems and the contemporary mechanisms by which books find their way into readers' hands (Olson 2007, 514). Book Industry Standards and Communication (BISAC) codes and the Dewey Decimal System (DDS) were established around information hierarchies that stem from syllogistic logic. There is an extensive body of research that examines the ways in which these hierarchies and systems of knowledge organisation are built upon White supremacist patriarchal structures (see, for example, Olson 2007; Adler and Harper 2018), and the radiating effects of these structures on societal perceptions and the maintenance of particular class dominance (see, for example, Noble 2018; Parnell 2022). Information hierarchies are structured so that 'the higher levels of the hierarchy define or have authority over the lower ones' (Olson 2007, 515). Critiques of this approach cite the fact that, for example, information relating to marginalised genders or races is nested under the seemingly more generic, and assumed White, 'man', implying a dichotomous, non-contradictory relational structure between men and not-men and between White and not-White people. These hierarchical relationships are also what structure the Amazon classification and recommendation algorithm and, therefore, play a significant role in the books that readers see when shopping on that platform.

Amazon's bookstore allows readers to browse millions of titles to find the book they're looking for. Purchases from Amazon account for around half of all print books and three-quarters of e-book sales in the United States, making the conglomerate e-retailer America's largest bookseller, as well as a major retailer in other markets (Anderson 2020). Convenience and abundance are perhaps the two features of Amazon's bookstore that are most attractive to readers. The problem with this abundance of titles, however, is finding something to read. Amazon's system of classification that underpins both the search and recommendation algorithms is designed to make finding the book you're looking for simple, and at the same time mimic the personalised shopping experience of staff recommendations that are intrinsic to the hand-selling practices in brick and mortar stores (Linden et al. 2003). The result is that one of the world's largest book retailers is organising book titles and authors according to a hierarchical classification system that, for example, classifies romance titles by White authors as romance fiction and romance titles by Black authors as Black romance fiction. Parnell's (2022) research into self-publishing platforms and authors who are marginalised along the lines of race and sexuality explores the Amazon algorithm and the ways in which it reinforces White supremacist structures, and demonstrates how when readers are searching for romance fiction on Amazon, they will primarily see the titles by White authors and the titles by Black authors will only be surfaced if they are specifically searched for. Similarly, if a reader purchases a romance title by a White author, their recommended titles list will preference other titles by White authors. Parnell (2022, 72) writes:

> Amazon's browse categories replicate acts of subjugation in traditional classification systems by designating literature by and about culturally marginalised groups as other from a 'General', unspecified but supposedly White, classification. In addition … Amazon uses profile data of authors, including author photos, biographies and metadata linked to other books from the same account, to determine how books should be categorised in its ecommerce system.

This demonstrates the coming together of the racist syllogistic logics of classification with the socially embedded perceptions of race, authority and knowledge acquisition to establish what Safiya Umoja Noble (2018) would call an 'algorithm of oppression'. In this way, the structure and operation of Amazon's bookstore and publishing platform are similar to the broader field of cultural production in that 'Those who have the power to design systems ... hold the ability to prioritize hierarchical schemes that privilege certain types of information over others' (Noble 2018, 138). The notion of the powerful possessing the privilege of designing the system is reminiscent of the system of structure-practice-structure that defines cultural production. Viewed through the lens of critical Whiteness studies, it is clear how the long-standing, unexamined acceptance of Whiteness as a generic or primary category of classification not only influences perceptions around subjects and people but also feeds into mechanisms by which books are sold and circulated. In turn, perceptions continue to be supported and reinforced by these mechanisms with every interaction.

From Literary Taste to the Book Marketplace

Amazon's bookstore offers a clear example of the relationship between established logics that underpin knowledge organisation and systems of classification, and the books that readers see, interact with and purchase in the Amazon ecosystem. This relationship is both an example and an expression of the logic of White taste in contemporary book culture. Beyond the Amazon platform, the structure and practices of White taste production that I have discussed in this chapter are often more difficult to identify and operate in a more insidious manner. In this way, the influence of White logics over the structure and practices of the contemporary publishing sector go largely under-examined and undetected, allowing this logic to remain unchallenged. However, in examining specific sites and sub-fields in contemporary book culture, the visibility of the consistent influence of this logic begins to appear. Just like So's study that reveals the overwhelming dominance of White authors among the list of most reviewed in American newspapers and magazines

(So 2021, 82), a similar dominance can be observed on the New York Times Bestseller list.

The logic of white literary taste is not confined to a specific corner of the field of production but influences the practice of book production, circulation and reception field-wide. This is evident in the repeated pattern of White dominance in almost every facet of contemporary book culture: publishing house staff, authors (published, most reviewed, prizewinning, bestselling), book critics and prize judges (Dane 2020c; Chowdhury 2021; Saha and van Lente 2022). The critical assessments made by book reviewers, the aesthetic judgements made by prize judges, the decisions made around algorithms that underpin the Amazon bookstore's functionality and the proclamations of bestseller status by the New York Times are all working within and perpetuating the continued existence of this logic. The bestseller list is perhaps the most pure confluence of professional and amateur tastemakers, and demonstrates the way that literary tastes are developed and cemented over time through interaction, discussion and attention. Some scholars suggest a linear relationship between critical attention and bestseller status (see, for example, Clement et al. 2007), however, I would suggest that this relationship is more complex than the simplistic explanation of 'word of mouth'. In exploring the symbiotic exchange between the bestseller and book culture, Helgason et al. (2014, 12) observe that 'bestselling fiction is not simply a sponge that absorbs ideological, cultural and aesthetic ideals that the reader can then wring from it, but it also has an impact on those ideals'.

The New York Times Bestseller lists publish the 'best selling' titles across a number of categories each week. The lists are built using sales figures reported from a 'panel of retailers' that represent bookstores both small and large across the United States (New York Times 2022a). Much has been written about the veracity of the Times' Bestseller lists and whether they reflect past or influence future sales (see, for example, Miller 2000; Sutherland 2007; Steiner 2014). Examining these lists is useful because they, in fact, simultaneously reflect and influence sales, and reveal the reception of authors and texts beyond the agents of consecration that more visibly mediate book culture. Moreover, these lists reveal the dominance of texts written by White authors in a pattern reminiscent of book reviews or literary prize shortlists (Figure 1).

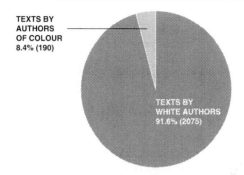

NYT FICTION BESTSELLERS: 2018-2020

TEXTS BY
AUTHORS
OF COLOUR
8.4% (190)

TEXTS BY
WHITE AUTHORS
91.6% (2075)

Figure 1 The proportion of texts by White authors versus the proportion of texts by authors of colour on the *New York Times* Hardback Fiction Bestseller Lists, 2018–2020.

Source: Pruett (2022)

Over the course of 2018, 2019 and 2020, 91.6 per cent of the books listed on the *New York Times*' hardback fiction bestseller list were written by White authors. Breaking this down year-on-year, titles written by White authors made up 91.4 per cent of the bestsellers in 2018, 94.3 per cent of the bestsellers in 2019 and 87.1 per cent of the bestsellers in 2020. In addition, texts written by White authors are also more likely than texts written by authors of colour to remain on the bestseller list for multiple weeks, as So (2021, 71) would say, 'racial inequality is resilient'.

Publishing's In Group and Publishing's Out Group

We can understand the logic of White taste in book culture to be based on assumptions around the identity of authors and readers and, perhaps more importantly, supported and perpetuated by the interrelated and interconnected nature of structure and practice. The operational disposition of Anglophone book culture runs throughout the sector, influencing book criticism, digital platform structural affordances and sales. Intrinsic to the continued survival of this logic is that it is only visible in its effects and that there is no single entity or individual or institution that can be transformed to bring about equality in the field. The upshot of this is that the focus for field-wide transformation is trained on individual action, the 'exchange of bodies and experiences' that Gray (2016, 246) describes.

The conception of who has the authority and legitimacy to be an author – not simply to write but to be an *author* – is deeply rooted in racist constructions about knowledge, knowledge production and authority. So too is the imagined audience for books. Saha and van Lente's (2022) research demonstrates the ways in which the image/identity of the reading public rarely shifts in the minds of publishers, despite evidence to the contrary. These two factors establish in and out groups in publishing that are structured around a White/not White dichotomy. We see the effects of this dichotomy in both professional and amateur practice in book culture. It is engrained in the way that critical consensus is formed in contemporary criticism, in the construction of the Amazon algorithm, in the books that readers buy en masse.

Over the next two chapters I will focus on two specific sites in contemporary book culture to explore the ways in which the logic of White taste plays out in two different sites in book culture: literary prizes and book discourse online. These two sites demonstrate the ways in which literary activism and projects for change fail to bring about the transformation they seek because of the way that the logic of White taste influences an inertia towards inequality.

3 White Feminist Solipsism and Women's Literary Awards

Literary prizes and awards are a highly visible form of promotion and celebration in the contemporary publishing sector. Increasingly from the 1930s, corporations, governments and well-endowed patrons of the arts have established literary prizes under the guise of selecting and exalting the very best books and the very best authors in order to enliven the literary field. Whether or not the ubiquity of literary prizes in contemporary book culture does, in fact, enliven the field or enrich literary participation remains a contentious subject, with much discussion within the scholarly literature around the utility, influence and effects of literary awards. Contemporary examinations of literary prizes and their influence often explore the ways in which these institutions exist as an integral part of the literary sector's structured hierarchy, where major literary awards confer to authors not just financial but also symbolic rewards (English 2005).

The late-twentieth and early-twenty-first centuries saw renewed attention paid to the relationship between gender and power in the publishing industry (see, for example, Zangen 2003; Lamond 2011; Squires 2013; Dane 2020c). The focus of much of the scholarly and media attention was gender equality and the representation of women authors in major book-reviewing publications and among the shortlisted and winning authors of major literary prizes. During this period, and in reaction to this attention, the Women's Prize for Fiction was established in the United Kingdom and the Stella Prize for Women's Writing was established in Australia. Both these prizes were conceived of as a way to subvert the dominance of male authors in the industry and challenge conventional ideas of literary prestige and traditional hierarchies of literary power. However, the founders, judges and administrators associated with both prizes appear to have failed to consider the ways in which literary power intersects with race (Kon-Yu 2016). In not explicitly accounting for the intersection of gender *and* race, these powerful literary institutions help to further obfuscate the dominance of Whiteness in the field.

In the study of this dominance and the racial inequities of the Anglophone publishing sector, prizes such as the Women's Prize and the Stella Prize offer a useful site for analysis of the different ways in which issues around equality are understood in the contemporary field. This chapter interrogates the questions of hierarchy, power and influence that have long been the focus of the study of literary prizes, moving beyond quantitative analyses of proportional representation, towards a more focused understanding of the mechanisms by which prizes – and the infrastructure that surrounds prizes – work to maintain this hierarchy. Two major women's literary prizes were established to challenge and transform field-wide male dominance; however, these institutions operate within and support a White feminist literary paradigm and, as a result, aid in supporting the dominance of White authors, and the logic of White taste, in the Anglophone literary field.

The ability of literary prizes to influence structures of power and notions of excellence within the publishing sector is built upon longevity, tradition and a field-wide belief in this ability (Dane 2020b). Individuals and institutions engaged in book culture – publishers, editors, authors, critics, booksellers, readers – all acknowledge the economic and symbolic power of the literary prize. Bourdieu (1993, 78) calls this the 'production of belief', a system wherein 'the value of works of art and belief in that value are continuously generated through the structured objective relations between institutions and individuals'. The value we place in literary prizes to consecrate authors and books, and to define the parameters of literary excellence, is established and continually re-established by the activities of the field that honour the belief in this value. In an exploration of contemporary literary awards, Claire Squires (2013, 299) observes the radiating power of the Booker Prize, noting that 'the next novel from a Booker Prize winner … will affect the whole of the publishing value chain, including the initial decision to publish'. Squires' observation illustrates the number of individuals and institutions that are involved in upholding this system of belief and the significant effects of this belief. What should not be overlooked in this examination of the power that prizes exert over the contemporary literary field is the very real, material impacts that accompany a literary prize shortlisting or win. Kara Locke (2017, 3) notes that for an author, the financial and economic ramifications of winning a prize 'can mean the freedom to continue writing and producing new work, the viability of a career'. It is the combination of both these effects – the lofty notions of literary excellence and celebration, coupled with the tangible outcomes and possibilities that the literary prize and the associated financial gains offers – that ensure that the literary prize is an enduring influence in the contemporary publishing sector, and that those operating within and beyond the literary field will continue to believe in it.

If the existence of the prize's influence is based upon a combination of belief in its power and the benefits of financial stability for authors, what, then, is the nature of this influence? Much of the scholarly research into the way prizes operate within a given field point to the judging panel and their decisions as individuals who have the privilege of determining notions of literary excellence and value (Norris 2006; Anand and Jones 2008; Driscoll 2014; Pouly 2016; Childress et al. 2017). Beth Driscoll's (2014, 128) research highlights the symbolic violence inherent in the act of judging a literary prize and selecting a winner, noting that the judging panel 'use their power to announce to the world which books are the most valuable'. Childress et al. (2017, 49) echo and extend this idea, observing the ways that the act of declaring literary winners not only aids in establishing but also 'reaffirms an underlying logic of distinction'. In this way the influence of literary awards and the nature of picking a winning title represents the syllogistic thinking that defines much of publishing industry practice. Driscoll's and Childress et al.'s. observations of the definitional power of literary prizes illustrate how the decisions of major literary awards influence the production, consumption and reception of literary works. Exploring this influence in light of the field's relational framework of practice–structure–practice (Bourdieu 1977) it is clear how a prize reinforces notions of value that are defined according to White taste logic and the racialised assumptions upon which the logic is based.

The definitional influence of contemporary literary prizes is often cited by critics of literary prizes who point to the conservative nature of the prize's power. Scholars examining literary prizes and notions of equality regularly point to the ways that prizes establish and re-establish the same parameters of literary excellence, based on homogenous and commonly held ideals. Sharon Norris (2006, 149) identifies the literary prize as a 'site of social reproduction', noting in relation to the Booker Prize that 'the [literary] values reproduced [by the judges' decisions] are invariably those of the dominant group' (157). Marie-Pierre Pouly (2016, 24) similarly explores dominant values established by dominant parties, observing that 'the dominant literary aesthetic code' can be understood 'by looking at the dominant cultural institutions that archive and stabilize literary value and transmit criteria of literary evaluation'. Women's literary prizes – institutions that have long championed notions of equality – bring to the fore a visible consciousness of this influence, and illustrate that the power that literary prizes confer to authors and publishers is steeped in historical inequities that have had enduring effects on the reception and circulation of women's writing (Dane 2020c; Stella Prize 2021). But it appears that both the institutional and much of the scholarly (see, for example, my work on gender in book culture (Dane 2020c)) reflections on this inequity typically refrain from extending this analysis to race.

The power and authority of the literary prize are explicitly linked to the ways in which they are covered by the mainstream media: the announcements of longlists and shortlists, judging panels and winners (English 2005, 215; Driscoll 2014, 134). This relationship has its foundations in the very purpose of literary prizes and the role that wide-spread visibility plays in the viability of the prize itself, and in the careers that the prize seeks to celebrate and promote (Driscoll 2014, 134). The cultural pages of major newspapers are integral to the popularization of the origin story of both the Women's Prize and the Stella Prize and cultural journalists and commentators have been equally as integral to the foundation and the continued visibility of both these institutions. As I will discuss in more detail in the forthcoming chapters, both the Women's and the Stella prizes were born out of a documented inequality in critical coverage and prize recognition between men and women authors (Stella Prize 2021; Women's Prize for Fiction 2021). This inequality was discussed in the book pages of the weekend newspapers (Mosse 1996; Groves 2015) and, as the two prizes came into being, the inequality continued to be discussed in relation to the annual activities of each prize (Stella Prize 2021). In this way, the media has been a vital institution for the ways in which gender inequality in the Anglophone literary field is framed and, therefore, broadly understood within and beyond the sector. Moreover, this analysis demonstrates how the media, and the cultural journalists covering book culture, support and affirm the logic of White taste through their coverage and framing of these awards, highlighting the pervasiveness of this practice across sectors of book culture.

Women's Literary Prizes in Contemporary Anglophone Book Culture

The historic conservative and homogenous nature of literary prize activity, and the ways in which this homogeneity flows through the publishing sector, was the impetus for the introduction of the Women's Prize in the United Kingdom in 1996 and the Stella Prize for Women's Writing in Australia in 2013. The origin stories for these two prizes are strikingly similar, a narrative that is evoked and repeated as a promotional tool in the mainstream media. These stories echo the themes explored in the previous chapter and have all the elements of a great feminist bookish story, with the imagery of 1970s feminist conscious-raising activities that centred around independent bookstores and literary communities (Travis 2008; Hogan 2016).

In 1992 a group of UK literary industry professionals – critics, publishers, booksellers and agents – got together in a flat in London to discuss whether or not it was a problem that no women authors were shortlisted for the 1991 Booker Prize. Founder and Director of the Women's Prize for Fiction, Kate Mosse writes:

> Everyone at that ad hoc first meeting was puzzled that, despite the ratio of books by men published to books by women being 60/40 in women's favour, the leading literary prizes nonetheless often seemed to overlook accomplished, challenging, important fiction by female authors … Did it matter? The group decided it did, since Prizes are an influential way of bringing outstanding writers to the attention of readers. (Women's Prize for Fiction 2021)

Mosse's recounting of the early days of the Prize is evocative: a group of industry insiders gathered in a small flat in London, drinking wine, debating the utility of literary prizes and the gender inequities that plague the industry. It is also an inspiring story, one where a group of people who are dissatisfied with the industry's deeply rooted inequalities band together to launch an exciting new project to bring about change. The combination of narrative and statistics – the ratio of published works by men versus women, the underrepresentation of women authors on the Booker Prize shortlist – is important for the way the prize is situated among the field of literary prizes in the publishing industry and provides a hook for attracting media attention. Early reporting on the Women's Prize for Fiction in the mainstream media regularly cited the prize's 'origin story' (Johnson 1996; Mosse 1996) and leant heavily on the statistical narrative. In an interview with Mosse in *The Guardian* in 1996, Joan Smith writes:

> Mosse immediately reels off facts and figures. In the past five years, out of the 29 authors shortlisted for the Booker, only four have been women … But what does this tell us? That women, who are often credited with seizing the novel and making it their own form in the 19th century, are no longer good at it? Mosse responded with a list of contemporary women writers who have never appeared on the Booker shortlist. (Smith 1996)

Smith (1996) goes on to reference the 'group of senior women in publishing' who thought the notion of another all-male Booker shortlist 'was too much', bringing together the two essential parts of the Women's Prize narrative. Reporting on the introduction of the prize in 1996, Angela Johnson (1996) cites the 1991 Booker Prize shortlist as the catalyst for the new Women's Prize, again cementing in the popular culture the literary prestige gender gap and the value of this new – and at the time somewhat controversial (Zangen 2003) – intervention.

The Stella Prize for Women's Writing was established within a very similar context, albeit almost a decade later. There are three pivotal events that underpin the establishment of the Stella Prize: a 2011 International Women's Day panel discussion at Readings Bookstore in Carlton, drinks and discussion at Markov (a now closed bar in Drummond Street, Carlton), and the 2011 all-male Miles Franklin Literary Award shortlist (Stella Prize 2021). For those who were involved in the founding of the Stella Prize, these are the common events that structure the narrative (Stella Prize 2021). Much like the Women's Prize, the Stella Prize was founded by a group of senior women in publishing – editors, authors, publishers, critics – who were troubled by the long-standing gender inequities that typified the Australian literary sector. The 2009 and 2011 all-male Miles Franklin literary award shortlists and the underrepresentation of women authors within the book review pages of major publications formed the foundation of the discussion between these women at Markov in March 2011. Jo Case, a Stella Prize co-founder, recalls that the group founded the prize to 'actively redress a recurring gender imbalance in local literary prizes and raise the profile of women writers' (Stella Prize 2021). Christine Gordon, another co-founder of the Stella Prize and participant in the International Women's Day event, writes about how the panel of speakers were unforgiving that night at Readings Carlton.

> Women authors were simply not getting enough attention in the media. Coverage was not equal. The more we listened to one another, the more our indignation grew … We knew that if we kept the conversation going we could instigate change. And so we did and the Stella Prize began. (Stella Prize 2021)

Again the inspiring combination of underrepresentation and collectivism underpins the creation of the prize. And again this narrative is taken up by the media and successfully used in the promotion of the award. Susan Wyndham (2013), reporting on the Prize's first shortlist in the *Sydney Morning Herald* in 2013, writes, 'The $50,000 prize, [was] started by a group of women writers to counter a perceived male bias in awards and media coverage.' Similarly, Jason Steger (2013) in *The Age* writes: 'When twice within the space of three years no woman was shortlisted for the Miles Franklin Literary Award, Australia's premier prize for fiction, a group of women in the books industry decided enough was enough: they would establish their own prize for writing – by women.' The media framing of the introduction of the prize speaks to the frustration of the Stella Prize founders and establishes the public justification for the action they took to transform the sector.

Today, discussion of gender and literary prizes appears to be a near-constant presence in the cultural pages of Australia's major newspapers and literary journals. Beginning around the time of the 2011 International Women's Day panel at Readings bookstore (which coincided with the release of the first VIDA count in the United States) and continuing to this day, public discussion around the gender prestige gap, the Stella Prize, the Women's Prize for Fiction and the perceived legitimacy of women's writing has not slowed. Writing on the topic of 'literary sexism' in the *Sydney Morning Herald* in 2012, critic Jane Sullivan explored the tacit perceptions of women's writing in the broader publishing field. Sullivan interviewed a number of prominent women in publishing about the subjugation of women's writing in the contemporary Australian publishing sector. Writer and critic Kerryn Goldsworthy observed to Sullivan that:

> Most of the unconscious bias I have seen in the literary world, and I have seen a great deal, has been to do with the male-centred values of a dominant culture whose values most people wrongly think are universal and gender neutral … most women share the values of the dominant culture, which is why it stays dominant and needs to be actively resisted. (Goldsworthy in Sullivan 2012)

Author Alison Croggon shared a similar view to Goldsworthy, noting:

> If millions of reinforcing signals say a women's work is less significant something will eventually begin to stick. This kind of intensifying feedback, which begins at birth, is very difficult to track and even more difficult to combat. (Croggon in Sullivan 2012)

Writing in the *Sydney Morning Herald* in 2015 about the 'gender bias against female authors', author and commentator Jane Caro cites both the gender gap in book reviews in Australia's major book reviewing publications, and the fact the continued practice of some women authors using their initials, rather than their perceived feminine first name, to promote the mission of the Stella Prize and contribute to the popular discourse around gender and literary prestige.

The discussion that has circulated through the cultural pages of Australia's major newspapers is rooted in and drawn from the discourse around gender and prestige explored in literary journals and magazines. Two essays published in 2011 have had a ripple effect on the structure of the conversation around women authors, literary prizes and book reviews. These two essays – by Stella Prize co-founder Sophie Cunningham writing in *Kill Your Darlings* and by Julieanne Lamond in *Meanjin* – structure their argument around quantitative data and notions of literary value and legitimacy, a framing that is visible in the subsequent op-eds and reporting in the newspapers. Cunningham writes:

> Women continue to be marginalised in our culture. Their words are deemed less interesting, less knowledgeable, less well-formed, less worldly and less worthy. The statistics are – in this humiliating and distressing matter – on my side. (Cunningham 2011)

Lamond similarly leans on notions of value and worthiness, writing:

> The marginalisation of women in various mechanisms for working out and rewarding literary value is nothing new. But in Australian literature, this has a history of its own ... There is a bias at work here, but it is a bias that is embedded in the structure of our thinking about the literary value, seriousness, importance, about gender difference, reading and writing. (Lamond 2011)

The problems around gender equality that Cunningham and Lamond identify here do exist, and notions of literary worthiness and the biases at play in the contemporary publishing sector manifest in a way where women's writing is disadvantaged. Moreover, this disadvantage goes beyond isolated perceptions of literary value and flows to systems of recognition that can influence the entire publishing process (Squires 2013). However, the ways in which the Women's Prize for Fiction, the Stella Prize for Women's writing – along with journalists, commentators, authors and scholars – frame the gender prestige gap do not adequately recognise the role that race also plays in the ways in which conceptions of value and 'worthiness' are established in the field, and the dominance of Whiteness when it comes to prestige, literary canon formation and the distribution of symbolic capital in the contemporary Anglophone publishing sector.

Women's Literary Prizes as an Expression of White Feminism

Women's literary prizes in Australia and the United Kingdom are good examples of the phenomenon of cultural redlining. So's analysis demonstrates that 'through every phase of the literary field ... White authors exercise a distinct racial command over minority authors, particularly Black novelists ... these numbers do not change over time' (2021, 3). The methodological approach that So (2021) undertakes in his research exists within a long-standing, albeit sporadic, tradition within the study of book cultures where quantitative descriptive demographic data informs an analysis of inequities in the publishing sector (see, for example, Cooter et al. 1987; Harvey and Lamond 2016; Dane 2020c). Moreover, this kind of research and this mode of inquiry was the reported catalyst for the launch of both the Women's Prize for Fiction and the Stella Prize for Women's Writing (Stella Prize 2021; Women's Prize for Fiction 2021). Where So's analysis differs from the work of Cooter, Harvey and Lamond, and myself is that the study starts with and foregrounds the issue of racial inequalities in the field, as opposed to gender inequalities. So does consider gender in his analysis but it is the systemic racism of the contemporary literary field that defines the study.

When examining literary recognition in the form of bestsellers and major literary awards, So's analysis reveals that White authors make up 98 per cent of the bestsellers and 91 per cent of the prizewinners between 1950 and 2000, a figure that does not change over the period (So 2021, 107, 108). As a point of contrast, my research into the relationship between gender and literary prestige from 1965 to 2015 reveals that on average over the fifty years to 2015, 38 per cent of the winners of seven major literary awards were women (Dane 2020c, 144–7). These data represent all women who won Australian literary prizes and although the data does not explicitly quantify author race the overwhelming majority of authors who won a literary award are White. I use my previous research here as a point of comparison with So's, to highlight the dominance of Whiteness in the post-war Anglophone literary field, as well as the dominance of Whiteness in my approach to the study of inequality in the literary field. My analysis does consider race but, in a reverse approach to So, only as a secondary analytical frame, foregrounding gender as if the experiences of the gender gap in the literary field is experienced by all women in an identical fashion.

In thinking about deep-seated inequalities around gender and race in the publishing industry, and the various interventions that have been introduced in order to transform dominant structures of power, it is helpful to look to scholars such as Kimberle Crenshaw (1989) and Aileen Moreton-Robinson (2000) to understand why research like my own, and literary prizes such as the Women's and the Stella Prizes, have done little to address field-wide racial inequities. In articulating the intersection of race and gender, Crenshaw identifies the 'single-axis framework' that dominates discourse around gender-based disadvantage. She writes:

> Dominant conceptions of discrimination condition us to think about subordination as disadvantage occurring along a single categorical axis … this single-axis framework erases Black women in the conceptualization, identification and remediation of race and sex discrimination by limiting inquiry into the experiences of otherwise-privileged members of the group. (Crenshaw 1989, 140)

Citing gender as the single axis upon which individuals are disadvantaged or subordinated within the contemporary literary field erases the real experiences of Black women and women of colour and by making Whiteness invisible serves to maintain the dominance of Whiteness. In *Talkin' Up to the White Woman: Indigenous Women and Feminism*, Moreton-Robinson observes how White feminist solipsism perpetuates the invisibility of race within feminist discourse, noting that:

> A universalist and essentialist construction of woman based on the promise that because all women are oppressed as women, this oppression must be the same … focussing on

power relations between white men and white women
means that their gaze is averted from analysing the power
relations between different women which prevent political
alliances. (Moreton-Robinson 2000, 54)

Both Crenshaw and Moreton-Robinson identify the whitewashing of
feminist approaches to transforming dominant patriarchal structures of
power, where explorations of dominance and power do not address the
multiple intersecting experiences of Black women and women of colour.
Moreton-Robinson (2000, 53) questions the assumptions that surround
White feminist practices wherein gender can be isolated from other aspects
of one's identity, noting that 'such an assumption underpins a dominant
White heterosexual feminist location because priority must be given to
overcoming gender oppression at the expense of other oppressions'.

Examining the establishment of and discourse around the Women's
Prize and the Stella Prize through the analytical lens of race-neutral or
White feminism that Crenshaw and Moreton-Robinson articulate brings the
presence of White feminist solipsism into sharp relief. The uncritical
reliance on broad gender-based statistics and the origin narratives for
both prizes – both factors popularised by the mainstream press – establishes
a rationale for the prizes that is rooted in the 'single-axis framework' that
characterises White feminist approaches to inequality. This approach to
transforming structures of power is limited in scope and often results in the
relocation of power in favour of White women while retaining the dominance of White people. Moreton-Robinson (2000, 42) observes that 'White
middle-class feminists utilise race privilege to write about their gendered
oppression, but whiteness remains invisible, unnamed and unmarked in
their work.' This is evident in the origin narratives that surround the
Women's Prize and the Stella Prize, where equality for women in the
field is championed without acknowledgement of the ways in which writers
of colour face a more stark marginalisation in the contemporary publishing
sector. The establishment of these two (and many other) prizes is based
upon the logic of White taste. The pervasiveness of this logic is evident in
the position and operation of the prizes in the contemporary literary field.

In the early years of the Women's Prize for Fiction (then known as the Orange Prize Fiction), there was a particular xenophobic tenor to the way in which the prize was reported in the mainstream media. In both 1997 and 1998 a non-British author won the Orange Prize, a fact that became a point of minor controversy. Writing in the *Guardian*, Dan Glaister (1997) called the winner, Anne Michaels, a 'rank outsider' and noted that the chair of judging panel 'provoked controversy in the run-up to last night's ceremony by siding with the Americans in the debate over the respective merits of British and American fiction'. Reporting on the shortlist for the 1998 Orange Prize in the *Guardian*, David Lister (1999) reminded readers that 'Last year the shortlist contained no English-born writers', noting that there was just one British novelist on the 1998 shortlist, 'Pauline Melville, who is half-Guyanese', and was born in Guyana. While this commentary is not explicitly or overtly racist, citing which shortlisted authors and winners are British and the number of 'English-born' authors is an unusual nationalistic framing for reporting on an international literary prize.

It is not, however, simply the mainstream media framing of the Women's Prize that operates within a framework of xenophobia and White feminism. In the first decade of the Women's Prize, there were only eight instances (12 per cent) where a woman of colour was shortlisted. Zadie Smith represents three of these instances, meaning that just five women of colour were shortlisted for the Women's Prize in the first 10 years it was awarded. There were also four years (1997, 2001, 2002, 2005) where every shortlisted author was White. This is particularly interesting given that the statistical rationale upon which the Women's Prize was established cites the years when no women were shortlisted for the Booker Prize. The first decade of the Women's Prize can be characterised by the practice that Moreton-Robinson describes, however, moving through the 2000s and into the late-2010s, there is a shift in the representation of authors of colour among the shortlistees, 38 per cent of the shortlisted works in the years 2016–2020 were written by authors of colour.

Moving beyond the early years of the Women's Prize – a period where single-axis thinking appears dominant – to the more contemporary era, the development of a greater consciousness of the Whiteness of the prize and the notion of feminist intersectionality is evident. For example, the inclusion of more women of colour on the prize shortlists: taking the first and second halves of the Prize's lifetime, the number of women of colour shortlisted for the Women's Prize almost doubled in the second period going from eleven in the first period to twenty-one in the second. Mariana Ortega (2006, 57) describes the 'loving, knowing ignorance', that characterises White feminism and its relationship to women of colour. A loving, knowing ignorance can be understood as 'an ignorance of the thought and experience of women of colour that is accompanied by both alleged love for and alleged knowledge about them'. This framework is useful for analysing the actions of contemporary women's literary prizes and flows from the thinking around White feminist solipsism that Audre Lorde (1984), Crenshaw (1989) and Moreton-Robinson (2000), among others, describe. However, even though the representation of women of colour on Women's Prize shortlists grew significantly over the period, twenty-one authors is just 27 per cent of the shortlisted authors in the years 2008–2020. Here we see the 'loving, knowing ignorance' at play. Ortega (2006, 57) writes:

> The desire, the great wanting of this [white] feminist is to be respected in a field that claims to care about women of colour and their thought. She sees herself as someone who really understands women of colour, who is putting the voices of these women on the map, who is 'giving' them a voice. She constructs a reality that is in fact closer to what she wants it to be rather than what it is – a reality in which the voices of women of colour are still taken seriously only if well-known white feminists quote them, in which white feminists who read the work of one woman of colour think they understand the experience of all women of color … in which women are seen as half-subjects who need to be 'given a voice' – hence loving, knowing ignorance.

The evolution of the Women's Prize towards the 'knowing, loving ignorance' is visible in the ways in which the prize describes itself. A 2003 version of the prize's website (then known as the Orange Prize) uses the prize's well-known origin tale as the explanation for the prize and its activities (Orange Prize for Fiction 2003). The 2020 iteration of the prize's website describes the Women's Prize as an organisation to 'empower all women to raise their voice and their own story', with the aim of 'shining a spotlight on outstanding and ambitious fiction by women from anywhere in the world, regardless of their age, race, nationality or background' (The Women's Prize for Fiction 2021). There is no mention of the early 1990s, large groups in small London flats or inequity on Booker Prize shortlists, rather there is an inspiring statement of inclusivity and celebration. This reads like a conscious narrative shift in response to calls for greater diversity. The proportion of authors of colour in the Women's Prize shortlists does not necessarily accord with the prize's contemporary self-description and is characteristic of the kind of White feminist approach that Ortega describes. This represents progress in some respects but there does not appear to be any effort to use the prize to transform the nature of equality more broadly in the sector.

A similar evolution can be seen in the Stella Prize. Writing about the Whiteness of the Australian publishing sector in 2016, Natalie Kon-Yu (2016) notes that since it was first awarded in 2013, the Stella Prize had 'come under increasing critique by women of colour about the whiteness of the prize's longlists'. The 2016 shortlist for the Stella Prize was made up exclusively of White women. Since 2016 there is evidence, both in the shortlists and in the ways in which the Prize discusses itself and its mission, that the issue of race and the Whiteness of the prize is a conscious factor at the organisation. The 2019 Stella Prize Judges' Report noted that, 'We wished for more representation of otherness and diversity from publishers: narratives from outside Australia, from and featuring women of colour, LGBTQIA stories, Indigenous stories, more subversion, more difference' (Stella Prize 2019). This is the first time that a statement of this nature, that acknowledges the underrepresentation of particular authors and particular stories, is made in an annual judges' report. Despite this acknowledgement, the evolution of both the Women's Prize and the Stella Prize is still rooted in a White feminist orthodoxy where, although the representation of women of colour is increasing, White women still dominate shortlists. Acknowledgements of racism, White-dominated spaces, and systematic inequalities in the literary field abound, but evidence of meaningful action is scant.

It is important to remember that the Whiteness of these mainstream literary prizes is just one part of the broader Whiteness of the contemporary Anglophone publishing industry. As discussed in Chapter 2 (Penguin Random

House 2021; Pham 2021), literary prizes act as a highly visible representation of the literary field, and they are institutions that are involved in selection, celebration and promotion of literary works and authors. What makes institutions like the Women's Prize and the Stella Prize important subjects of analysis is the fact that notions of equality and the redistribution of power are core to their existence. At the same time, however, the work of a literary prize is inherently bound up in the symbolic violence of selecting winners. This gatekeeping function is characteristic of White feminist practice and can be observed in the profile of the shortlists and judging panels, and while evolution and attempts to be more inclusive is evident at both the Women's Prize and the Stella Prize, the logics of White taste that form the foundations of the prizes remain. Over the twenty-five-year history of the Women's Prize for fiction, there have been ten years where the entire five-person judging panel was White, thirteen years where the panel had just one person of colour and two years where there were two people of colour on the panel. Writing on the privileges of the contemporary White feminist, Ortega (2006, 68) writes:

> Such privileges include being the one who decides which women of colour gets to be let into the club, being able to speak for women of colour, being able to feel that she is the one responsible for their salvation, and having the voice to see women of colour or not.

In his exploration of cultural redlining, So (2021, 78) describes the 'Toni Morrison Effect'. The Toni Morrison Effect is the notion that 'literary gatekeepers … appear *very* interested in *certain* Black authors' (So 2021, 81) (original emphasis) and that '*when* the literary gatekeepers admit Black authors into the literary 1 percent, they do so with very specific rules of inclusion . They will only distribute their attention in highly unequal terms, favouring specific single authors, like Morrison' (So 2021, 82). The Toni Morrison Effect is a constant factor in both the British and the Australian publishing industries and plays out in the Women's Prize and the Stella Prize. I argue that, in the United Kingdom, author Zadie Smith is entangled in the Toni Morrison Effect. I make this argument not to take anything away from Smith's literary achievements or impact, but to demonstrate the ways in which the

Women's Prize continues to operate from a White taste logic. Smith is among a very small group of authors of colour who are sometimes used by institutions like literary prizes to show that they are diverse or inclusive. Earlier I cited the four years where only White women were shortlisted for the Women's Prize (1997, 2001, 2002, 2005). In addition to these four years, there are another four years wherein the only woman of colour shortlisted for the prize was Smith: 2000, 2003, 2006 and 2013. Waanyi author Alexis Wright, the first author of colour to win the Stella Prize, could be considered the Australian publishing industry's manifestation of the Toni Morrison Effect: Wright has won numerous accolades, however, these achievements do not represent a transformation in the field nor a reckoning about the continued dismissal of the work of First Nations authors and authors of colour by White dominated publishers and literary institutions. The Toni Morrison Effect is a manifestation of the logic of White taste in contemporary book culture, and it plays out clearly in the arena of literary prizes and awards. Individual authors become the focus of efforts on the part of mostly-white institutions to bring about diversity and inclusion, an individualistic approach that is guaranteed to not disrupt the dominance of the dominant class.

Examining racism, diversity and institutions, Sara Ahmed (2012) interrogates notions of inclusivity and the discourses around institutional diversity. While Ahmed's study is focused on Universities, it is useful for exploring the relationship between Whiteness and literary institutions such as the literary prize. The supremacy of Whiteness at the Women's Prize and the Stella Prize is *more* than just the statistical breakdown of White women versus women of colour. And while White women dominate the shortlists – 80 per cent of authors shortlisted for the Women's Prize and 70 per cent of the authors shortlisted for the Stella Prize are White women – the history of both prizes and the ways in which both prizes have evolved over time indicate that primarily these prizes were conceived of for White women authors and notions of diversity and inclusivity have been brought in over time. Ahmed (2012, 33) contends that it is this kind of logic that works to 'keep whiteness in place', and that 'if diversity becomes something that is added to organizations … then it confirms the whiteness of what is already in place'. Ahmed goes on to note that for predominantly White institutions working towards greater inclusivity, 'Diversity becomes about changing perceptions of whiteness rather than changing the whiteness of organisations' (2012, 34). The twenty-five-year history of the Women's Prize, the historic profile of the shortlists and the judging panels, supports the argument that the Women's Prize is not an organisation that aims to transform the profile of power in the contemporary literary field, rather, is an organisation working to change the perception of White literary institutions. Additionally, the piece-meal nature of racial inclusivity is such that instead of bringing about equality in the publishing industry, it is used as a substitute for genuine, long-term evolution. Writing on displays of inclusivity in academic institutions, Ahmed (2012, 34). observes that, 'When our [people's of colour] appointments and promotions are taken up as signs of organizational commitment to equality and diversity, we are in trouble. Any success is read as a sign of overcoming institutional whiteness.' A similar observation can be made of the Women's Prize and the Stella Prize in their approach to racial equity. Herein lies the central issue of the prize as a tool for bringing about industry change. Appointments and promotions of authors and their work are the core function of prizes and the inherent symbolic violence of these practices means that prizes are limited in their transformative abilities.

Equality for Who?

Little meaningful change has eventuated and the shortlists of major literary awards are still dominated by White authors. Women's literary prizes occupy an interesting position in these debates and discussions as their existence is based upon a logic of gender equality, however, as I have explored in this chapter, this logic does not address the intersection of gender and race and, therefore, approaches the issue of inequality from a perspective of White feminist solipsism. Women's literary prizes are just one part of a complex and dynamic Anglophone literary field that seeks to uphold racist hierarchies of power. What makes them an interesting and important site of study is their stated progressive ideologies and signals towards equality. By stating so prominently – on prize promotional materi-als, in the mainstream media, at prize-giving events – their commitment to equality, women's literary prizes make opaque the role they play in sup-porting the dominance of Whiteness in the contemporary publishing sector.

4 The Transformative Limits of the Anti-Racist Reading List

The circulation of anti-racist reading lists – lists of books that focus on the topic of race and racism, typically but not always written by Black authors – gained significant momentum on social networking platforms like Instagram and Twitter alongside Black Lives Matter protests in 2020, and continue to feature in the pop cultural and social media discourse around systemic racism and White supremacy in countries such as Australia, the United States and the United Kingdom. June 2020 saw a surge in the circulation of anti-racist reading lists featuring titles such as titles *White Fragility* (2018) by Robin DiAngelo, *How to Be an Antiracist* (2019) by Ibram X Kendi and *Why I'm No Longer Talking to White People About Race* (2017) by Reni Eddo-Lodge. These titles all became international bestsellers. Anti-racist reading lists, and the books they recommend, form part of the online discourse around racism where people, and in particular White people, are encouraged to listen, read and learn about historic and contemporary systems that perpetuate racism in order to combat their own ingrained biases and fight to transform bigoted and exclusionary structures.

The existence of and discourse surrounding these reading lists gives rise to a number of questions around race in contemporary book culture, the different methods used to dismantle systemic racism, as well as the role of books, authors and readers in this process. The popularity of anti-racist reading lists on social media also inspires questions about the effectiveness of the circulation of such lists and the public discussion of books by Black authors on social media, and the ways in which posting a stack of books on Instagram, with the implication of reading, can act as a kind of progressive veneer for White people, allowing them to appear responsive to Black voices in the pursuit of equality without making any real changes. This performance can be understood as a kind of 'digital spectator activity', a classification of clicktivism that achieves varying levels of impact (George and Leidner 2019, 8). Posting a list of titles about systemic racial injustice on Twitter and encouraging your followers to read these titles does little to confront the logic of White taste that underpins the racial inequality that characterises the publishing sector.

The popularity of anti-racist reading lists on social networking platforms, together with the discussion of anti-racist reading lists in literary magazines and news publications (Jackson 2020; Saad 2020), highlights the continuing role of the book as a foundation for cultural discourse and the ways in which individuals on platforms like Twitter and Instagram use the book as a tool for generating discussion and signalling cultural capital. However, beyond this, these lists illustrate the ways in which genuine discussion and protest around racial inequality distils in book culture, and how calls for self examination and structural interrogation manifest in ways that do little to disrupt White hegemony in contemporary Anglophone publishing sectors.

In this chapter, I articulate the relationship between the anti-racist reading lists, the books that regularly appear on the lists, the discourse surrounding the lists and the ways in which White people use the lists to signal particular liberal values. I explore questions around the expectations and the realities of anti-racist reading lists in a Black Lives Matter age, as well as the possibilities and limitations that posting anti-racist reading lists on Twitter and Instagram present. Does the circulation of reading lists and the discussion of Black-authored books by White people contribute to the dismantling of societal racial intolerance and White supremacy, or is this simply a carefully curated distraction? What role does the book play in contemporary discussions of race and equality on social media platforms? Can highlighting the writing of Black authors and authors of colour bring about structural changes in the publishing industry and challenge the logic of White taste that informs industry practice?

The rationale behind the circulation of anti-racist reading lists is that if people can learn about systemic racism and the enduring presence of white supremacy by reading the experiences of Black people and people of colour, they will work to dismantle the long-standing structures that support inequality. This rationale rests upon two assumptions. The first is the idea that if White people read and understand the experiences of Black people, they will be inspired to enact change. This relies upon the perceived power of reading to build empathy, however, the research into the effects of reading on empathy, and the relationship between empathy and knowledge, fails to reach a consensus. Perhaps more importantly, the second assumption embedded in the presumption of the power of the anti-racist reading list is the idea that everyone who creates and shares a list of Black authored books has or will read the books on the list. Can systemic inequality be transformed if White social media users are sharing lists as a way to signal their accumulated cultural capital (Dane 2020a)? I consider these questions over the course of this chapter, exploring the assumed connection between empathy and reading, the values that underpin the practice of sharing anti-racist reading lists, and examining the titles that commonly appear on anti-racist reading lists and what they can tell us about the structures of inequality that underpin Anglophone book culture.

The Transformative Power of Reading?

Research into the transformative power of reading and the ability of books to make us more moral or empathic people is inconsistent and there does not appear to be a common consensus around the ability for books to build empathy. Small groups of literary scholars and cognitive scientists alike have hypothesised the ways in which reading the experiences of others (in both fiction and non-fiction) can help a reader to build empathy for others and, in turn, live lives in a more moral way (see, for example, Landy 2012; Vezzali et al. 2014). Tentative links have been made by scholars between the rise in literacy rates during the eighteenth century and 'expanding empathy to humanity' (Decety 2014, 338), however, history tells us that there is a limit to the extent of this expansion in empathy. Perhaps the most well-known of the contemporary studies into the link between reading, 'out-group experiences', as they are known, and building empathy in readers is a 2015 study published in the Journal of Applied Social Psychology where the link between reading *Harry Potter* and increased 'out-group' empathy is supported (Vezzali et al. 2014). The researchers found that, 'people form attitudes not only by conforming to positive relevant others, but also by distancing themselves from negative relevant others' (115), supporting the notion that if White readers read books by racially marginalised authors about the experiences of racially marginalised people, they will individually build more positive attitudes to the traditionally marginalised group. This extrapolated finding is the rationale that underpins the sharing of anti-racist reading lists across social media platforms.

Taking a step away from cognitive science and social psychology, there is an argument to be made about the role of reading and learning in the course of living a life characterised by empathy for others. While there is temptation to lean on studies about neural pathway development and the complex psychology of identity, identification and the evolution of attitudes, in the context of the anti-racist reading list it is perhaps better or more useful to consider the connection between reading and the desire to learn about and understand the experiences of others. The framing of this, however, is explicitly connected to the logic of White taste in that it is established around the assumptions of who constitutes a reading public, and also places writing by Black authors and authors of colour into an educative role that specialises in the topic of race, separate and apart from the 'general' category of (assumed White) authors who have the authority and accumulated legitimacy to write on any subject. This is not to say that those authors of colour who are writing about race and experiences of structural racism are not doing so with authority and legitimacy, but that within the context of broader book culture, White-led discourses around anti-racist reading lists and the process of 'doing the work' – that is, learning about and enacting the tactics and strategies for being explicitly anti-racist – are conducted in line with the logic of White taste and therefore place this writing in a separate sub-category.

This framing is particularly prevalent in the life writing genres. Research into the life writing and autobiography written by Black Americans from the mid-twentieth century illustrates how non-fiction (and in particular autobiographical texts) have long been viewed by White readers as pedagogical aids. And while this experience will differ for Black readers and for readers of colour, it is important to keep in mind the assumptions that publishers, reviewers and critics make about the identity of reading public (Chowdhury 2021). Writing in 1974, Stephen Butterfield (1974, 1) observes that:

> Any good autobiography does two things for the reader:
> affirms his [sic] potential worth, and calls his realization of
> that worth into question by telling a true story of someone

who has travelled a different path. Black autobiography does these two things for our whole civilization. Black writers offer a model of the self which is different from white models, created in response to a different perception of history and revealing divergent, often completely opposite meanings to human actions.

The tradition of Black life writing in America, exemplified by texts such as James Baldwin's *Notes of a Native Son* (1955) and Maya Angelou's *I Know Why the Caged Bird Sings* (1969), suggests that non-fiction, and in particular the life writing genres, have long been a popular way to tell Black stories to both Black and to White audiences. Scholars of life writing illuminate the ways in which autobiography afforded Black writers the opportunity to write Black history and that autobiography was the way that many Black authors entered, or were permitted to enter, the White-dominated publishing industry (Olney 1980, 15). This exclusion is rooted in the assumptions around authority and literary legitimacy I explore in Chapter 2, wherein there exists the tacit assumption that an author is White man and an author who does not fit this dominant classification is defined within a sub-classification. Butterfield's research into the cultural history of Black autobiography in America identifies a position that this writing occupies within its contemporary publishing sector that is similar to that which we see today. He observes, 'Major publishers usually have shown interest in Black stories only when race became a national issue and the political struggles of black people could not be ignored' (1974, 5). Butterfield's observation is reminiscent of the increase in the public attention paid to Black authors in the wake of the 2020 Black Lives Matter protests. While this increased attention to life writing by Black authors and authors of colour is not unique to our current moment, social networking technologies and the categorisation possibilities that hashtags afford makes this practice visible.

The sharing of anti-racist reading lists on Twitter and Instagram, commonly accompanied by images of book covers or 'reading stacks', illustrates a very individual or individuated approach to a society-wide structural problem. And, in sharing a reading list, a social media user creates a relationship between themselves, the titles and authors on the reading list, and their followers. Particularly where White readers/social media users are concerned, these lists are deeply symbolic and recall a certain set of values that took root in the period of eighteenth-century Western European Enlightenment where ideas around progression and humanity were sought through the sharing of knowledge. The existence of the anti-racist reading list indicates that these ideas and values and the continual pursuit of self-knowledge, self-improvement and self-actualisation persist in post-digital book culture (Pressman 2020, 33).

Marielle Macé (2013, 216, 218) observes the transformative possibilities of reading, and argues that reading is a practice that encourages individuals to examine the self and the distance between the self and the text. The act of reading, Macé argues, 'forces us to reassess our dispositions' and the environment within which we and our dispositions exist (2013, 226). The power to change individuals and even environments in this way appears to be dependent on deeply engaging with a book. Anti-racist reading lists might encourage or promote the practice of reading in this way but the sharing of these lists on social networking platforms is not itself an act of deep engagement. And while sharing a list of books on social media is not the same as reading, it is a practice that is essential to contemporary book culture – discussing books online, posting images of 'TBR' piles, buying and recommending books, engaging with authors and other readers on social media – and so in a small way represents a minor or surface engagement with the text. This might appear at first superficial, and in the truest sense of the word it is, however, sharing anti-racist reading lists does make a contribution to the ways in which readers will connect with a text and how these texts are situated and contextualised. And while this situating and contextualisation might not bring about the desired structural changes or upend racial inequality, it does add to the cultural framing and under-standing of both text and reader.

Macé describes the possibilities that reading affords for a transformative relationship between both reader and the aesthetics of a text, and between reader and the aesthetics of their environment (2013, 219). The intensity of the impact of an author and a book is made possible through engagement with the text and an understanding of how the text is contextually situated. What, then, is the aesthetic engagement – 'the pas de deux of every aesthetic relationship', as Macé (2013, 19) describes it – that occurs between reader, text and their environment when engagement is superficial and the discourse that flows from the engagement on social media is less about the text itself but the symbol that the text represents?

Cultural Capital, Bookstagram and White Progressive Performativity

It is helpful to again look back to the underpinnings of the logic of White taste, and the assumed in-group/out-group dynamics of authors and readers upon which this logic is structured. As noted in Chapter 2, Ramdarshan Bold (2019), Chowdhury (2021) and Saha and van Lente (2022) all explore the ways in which publishers base their editorial decisions on assumed White identity of their reading public, however, focusing solely on publishers and not other intermediaries obscures the ways in which this logic is embedded in every facet of Anglophone book culture. As explored in the introduction to this volume, when Faber & Faber tweet a long list of titles with an aim 'to help educate on racism and white privilege and what you can do to help enact change' (Faber 2020), they are not speaking to Black readers or readers of colour, they are speaking to their assumed audience of White readers. And while the onus of transforming the structures and logics of systemic racism is on White people, the generalised framing of Faber & Faber's tweet, which speaks to their whole audience and does not single out their White readers, reveals an assumption about who they envisage their readers to be.

While the posting of anti-racist reading lists on social media platforms is not a practice that is inherently racially coded, this practice does adopt a particular veil of performativity where White posters are concerned. This performativity speaks to the notion of accumulating and communicating cultural capital, where knowledge of and interaction with particular cultural objects and practices denotes particular group affiliation (Bourdieu 1984, 94). In the context of our interconnected and platformatised lives, it is not just cultural practices but also making public connections and associations with political discourses that signals a quasi-cultural capital: sharing an anti-racist reading list on Twitter or Instagram makes an explicit tie between the poster and book culture, an educative reading practice that recalls

Enlightenment ideals and access to leisure time, and a liberal or progressive political affiliation that is so commonplace in book culture. The ways in which this accumulated capital is signalled and communicated differ depending on the situational context. For the White liberal bookish community on Twitter and Instagram, performing race allyship is an important component of communicating capital. It is for these reasons that since May 2020 '#antiracistreadinglist' has exploded online and is now associated with hundreds of thousands of posts on Twitter and Instagram.

The notion of knowing, loving ignorance that commonly characterises White feminism is a useful framework to understand both the roots of and the effects of the sharing of these reading lists. The sharing of anti-racist reading lists by White people on social media platforms is a practice that can be understood as existing within the context of third-wave feminism and calls for intersectional approaches and considerations within the feminist movement (Lorde 1984; Hill Collins 2019). And while posting these reading lists may, superficially, respond to a perceived need to be 'inclusive' or to 'amplify' the voices of Black authors and authors of colour, interrogation of this social media trend indicates a less revolutionary impetus on the part of the White list-posters. Ortega (2006) theorises White feminism as being 'lovingly, knowingly ignorant' of the intersecting issues of race and gender that women of colour experience. I find this framing helpful for the analysis of the practice of posting anti-racist reading lists on social media as it brings together the motivation, affect and effect that is tied up in the act of posting these lists.

The two Instagram posts in Figures 2 and 3 display all the hallmarks of the loving, knowing ignorance that Ortega describes, where authors of colour are cited and amplified but no rigorous engagement, interrogation or analysis is required on the part of the poster or the reader. And while examining this from the outside reveals not only this superficiality but also the inherent ignorance that is embedded in this practice, within the two-way interaction between a White person posting an anti-racist reading list on Instagram and their White follower reading the book titles on the list – and even perhaps going so far as to purchase books on the list – a moment of recognition of conspicuous consumption and, therefore, a signalling and an exchange of cultural capital occurs (Dane 2020a, 24). This micro interaction

Figure 2 Instagram post and caption categorised under the hashtag #antiracistreadinglist

illuminates the ways in which these lists, when posted by White people, make 'half-subjects' (Ortega 2006, 64) out of Black authors and authors of colour and centre the experiences of the White people 'giving a voice' to authors of colour.

This practice elicits three major outcomes. First, the perceived or assumed benevolence of the collective sharing an anti-racist reading list

Figure 3 Instagram post and caption categorised under the hashtag #antiracistreadinglist

on social media contributes to the production of a collective constructed knowledge about the experiences of people of colour (Ortega 2006, 64). The thousands of #antiracistreadinglist posts on social media, sharing the work from hundreds of Black authors and authors of colour, works to ring-fence the experiences of these authors and the subjects they write about so that this writing is *the* example of writing by Black authors and authors of colour, leaving little space for other forms of writing (Saha 2016, 183). Building upon this first outcome, the second outcome is the reinforcement of the imagined reading public as White. As previously discussed, it is not just White people sharing these lists, however, they were typically shared for the benefit of White people. And while it is understandable that White people would be the target audience for lists of this nature, the result is that in the radiating discourse around racism, books and reading that has taken root in book culture amid ongoing Black Lives Matter protests, it is White readers who occupy the space. Finally, the third outcome from the sharing of these lists is that sharing anti-racist reading lists, posting about reading titles that commonly feature on the lists, has become a short-hand for 'doing the work' of being anti-racist, without actually doing 'the work'. However, this kind of posting is a kind of promotional labour that ultimately benefits the publishing industry. In Figure 2, the poster outlines their ant-racist 'goals' alongside their reading recommendations. They state that they will:

1. center non-white voices in my life
2. open my eyes to the racism that exists in the world and in my heart, and
3. fight it.

The goals that this Instagram user publishes alongside their anti-racist reading list are worthwhile, however, just like the reading lists themselves, they require no real meaningful action or change on the part of the poster or the reader. In this way the White people posting book recommendations on Instagram amplifying the work of Black authors and authors of colour are able to remain lovingly, knowingly ignorant. The posting of these lists recalls the actions of consciousness raising and knowledge acquisition (Travis 2008), however, this performance signals to knowledge acquisition without evidence of increased consciousness.

The Influence of the Anti-Racist Reading List on the Bestseller List

In order to understand the influence of the anti-racist reading list beyond the social media discourse, I looked again to the *New York Times* bestseller lists. As discussed in Chapter 2, analysing weekly bestseller lists is a useful way to observe the coming together of professional and amateur tastemaking, and how these two often distinct groups come together in the bestseller list to both reflect and influence contemporary book culture (Helgason et al. 2014, 12). In the context of the rapid growth in sharing anti-racist reading lists on Twitter and Instagram from late-May 2020, examining the bestseller lists can offer insights into not only the ways in which these lists may have influenced book buying in the United States, but also the radiating and lasting effects of this influence. Is the amplification of marginalised voices by White social media users having any effect on book culture?

I analysed data from *New York Times* hardback fiction and non-fiction weekly bestseller lists for the months of May, June and July in 2020 and 2021. I took this approach as I was interested in understanding if there was any relationship between the sharing of anti-racist reading lists and the list of bestsellers, if this relationship changed over time and if the sharing of mostly non-fiction and autobiographical titles by Black authors had any influence on the sales of fiction titles by Black authors and authors of colour.

There was a marked increase in the proportion of bestselling non-fiction titles by authors of colour over the sample period in 2020 (Figure 4). Titles by authors of colour constituted just 21 per cent of titles on the list in the week of 3 May, but by late June, there was a fairly even split between bestselling non-fiction titles by White authors and by authors of colour. This pattern does not appear to have sustained into 2021 other than for three weeks in late-June and early-July 2021 (Figure 5). These data suggest that there was a meaningful but not sustained relationship between the 2020 Black Lives Matter protests (and the sharing of anti-racist reading lists that form a part of the movement) and non-fiction book sales. Examining the titles on the bestseller lists can provide additional insight into this relationship.

The representation of Black authors and authors of colour on the 2020 hardback non-fiction *New York Times* bestseller list saw a marked change throughout the sample period. In May 2020, the non-fiction titles by Black authors on the bestseller list were memoirs by high-profile individuals – *Becoming* by Michelle Obama, *The Mamba Mentality* by Kobe Bryant, *More Myself* by Alicia Keys, *24: Life Stories and Lessons from the Say Hey Kid* by Willie Mays, *The Chiffon Trenches* by Andre Leon Tally – and pop-philosophy title *Talking to Strangers* by Malcolm Gladwell. However, by

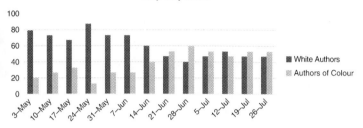

Figure 4 *New York Times* hardback non-fiction bestsellers, 3 May–27 July 2020.
Source: New York Times (2022b)

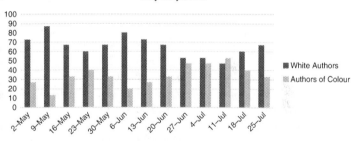

Figure 5 *New York Times* hardback non-fiction bestsellers, 2 May–25 July 2021.
Source: New York Times (2022c)

the second week in June there was a distinct change, with the appearance of titles that focused explicitly on racism and White supremacy. Layla F Saad's *Me and White Supremacy* (2020) and Ibram X Kendi's *How to Be an Antiracist* (2019) were the first two titles in this genre to feature on the list and both titles remain bestsellers throughout the sample period. These two titles were joined on the list by Ta-Nehisi Coates' *Between the World and Me* (2015), Austin Channing Brown's *I'm Still Here: Black Dignity in a World Made for Whiteness* (2018) and Mikki Kendall's *Hood Feminism: Notes from the Women White Feminists Forgot* (2020) throughout June and July. What is particularly striking is the mix of new-release and slightly older titles on the list, indicating the potential influence of the discussion of anti-racist books on the bestseller list. *How to Be an Antiracist*, *Between the World and Me* and *I'm Still Here* were all published between 2015 and 2019. These three titles are commonly cited on anti-racist reading lists posted on Twitter and Instagram by both publishers and readers.

This trend continues in 2021, with 35 per cent of the non-fiction titles by Black authors and authors of colour (and 12 per cent of all titles in the 2021 sample) on the bestseller lists taking White supremacy and systemic racism as their focus: *Caste: The Origins of Our Discontents* (2020) by Isabel Wilkerson, *How the Word Is Passed: A Reckoning with the History of Slavery Across America* (2021) by Clint Smith, *On Juneteenth* (2021) by Annette Gordon-Reed and *The Sum of Us: What Racism Costs Everyone and How We Can Prosper Together* (2021) by Heather McGhee. What is perhaps most revealing about these lists, and their relationship to the discourse around anti-racist books, is that the dominant theme of the overwhelming majority of the bestselling non-fiction titles by Black authors and authors in both the 2020 and 2021 sample period is race and White supremacy, a change that came about from late-May to mid-June 2020. Over the 2021 sample period, it is perhaps only *The Bomber Mafia* (2021) and *Talking to Strangers* (2020) by Malcolm Gladwell, *The United States of Socialism* (2020) by Dinesh D'Souza and *What Happened to You* (2021) by Oprah Winfrey and Bruce D Perry where race is not explicitly discussed. On the other hand, titles by White authors on the non-fiction bestsellers list explore a much more diverse range of subjects: Winston Churchill, escaping a fundamentalist church through education, modern monetary theory, politics, military history, becoming friends with a fox, the Anthropocene in the current geological age, the Trump administration and cognition in decision-making are among the topics explored in the bestselling non-fiction by White authors during the two periods studied. This extends

So's (2021, 82–3) exploration of the relationship between Black authors and book reviewing culture wherein a very small number of Black authors attract consistent and sustained critical attention in the major American reviewing publications, and, on the other hand, a large variety of White authors are afforded sustained attention by critics and reviews. Data from these bestseller lists suggest that although the Black Lives Matter movement and anti-racist reading lists on social media may have influenced a rise in title sales for books about race and White supremacy, both professional and amateur tastemakers have a limited imagination or conception of what Black authors and authors of colour have the accumulated authority or legitimacy to write about, a limitation not placed on White authors.

Did the increase in sales for non-fiction titles by Black authors and authors of colour flow beyond non-fiction into broader book culture? Data from the hardback fiction *New York Times* bestsellers lists for May, June and July in 2020 (Figure 6) and in 2021 (Figure 7) would suggest that there is no correlation between the calls to amplify Black voices and Black-authored books and the proportion of Black authors or authors of colour on the fiction bestseller lists.

Fiction titles by White authors dominate the *New York Times* fiction bestseller lists, with very few titles by Black authors and authors of colour. Unlike non-fiction titles, there appears to be no major connection between anti-racist reading lists and fiction bestsellers, illuminating the transformative limits of the sharing of these lists for broader book culture. These data bring to mind hooks' observation of the invisible annual quota for fiction by Black women (1989, 143) and scholarship on the history of Black life writing explored earlier in this chapter. History and autobiography/memoir were traditionally the genres where Black authors and authors of colour were afforded more opportunities from the almost exclusively White publishing houses and institutions (Olney 1980; So 2021, 82). The upshot of this, as Butterfield (1974) observes, is that the almost exclusively White publishing houses and institutions turned their attentions to Black authors writing history and autobiography during times when the issues of race and White supremacy garnered attention from the mainstream media and, therefore, circulated through White-dominated cultural and social spaces. In considering the nature of the publishing sector and contemporary book

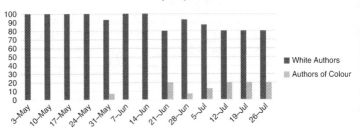

Figure 6 *New York Times* hardback fiction bestsellers, 3 May–27 July 2020. Source: Pruett (2022)

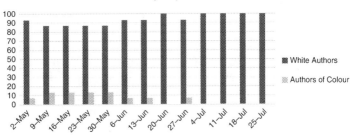

Figure 7 *New York Times* hardback fiction bestsellers, 2 May–25 July 2021. Source: New York Times (2022d)

culture – the generative practice–structure–practice relationship is the foundation of activity, the roots of the practice of posting an anti-racist reading list on social media, and the critical and popular attention for titles such as Austin Channing Brown's *I'm Still Here: Black Dignity in a World*

Made for Whiteness (2018) and *Caste: The Origins of Our Discontents* (2020) by Isabel Wilkerson – together with the scholarship on Black life writing, it becomes clear why the increase in the proportion of Black authors and authors of colour on the non-fiction bestseller list might not have translated to a similar rise on the fiction list.

This is not to say that the work of Clint Smith, Ta-Nehisi Coates, Layla F Saad and Ibram X Kendi are not vital to book culture and broader societal discussions, or that publishers should overlook contemporary writing that examines entrenched structural White supremacy. However, these non-fiction bestseller lists and the discrepancy between the non-fiction and the fiction lists are an example of the White taste logic at play – who is/is not an author, who is/is not a reader – and demonstrate how this logic that underpins professional practice in the publishing sector radiates out into broader book culture. Within the publishing sector, professional practice operates within the framework of this logic, which in turn influences the broader book culture and the practice of readers. Anti-racist reading lists are also constructed within the framework of this logic, taking the books published by industry and framing them in a way that reinforces the logic.

Anti-Racist Reading Lists and the Economies of the Bestseller

For White people, reading books written by Black authors can be viewed as being part of building an anti-racist practice. This is not something that originated with the Black Lives Matter movement and is rooted in ideas developed within the Enlightenment as well as the consciousness-raising that often underpins expanding social and civil rights movements (Travis 2008). 2020, however, saw an explosion of content online that centred around promoting books written by Black authors and authors of colour. The contemporary anti-racist reading list shared on social media typically accompanies discussions about White people educating themselves on the systemic racism that structures society in countries like the United States, the United Kingdom and Australia and there have long been calls from people both within and outside the field of publishing and cultural production for an amplification of the work by authors of colour. These discussions, which play out on social media platforms like Twitter and Instagram, often focus on not only the transformative power of reading but also speak to the possibility of a commercial or economic reality that does not exist. Saha's (2016, 11) examination of the racialised logics that underpin book production illustrates that contemporary Anglophone book production does not simply operate within a structure of supply and demand, and that calls from readers for more books by authors of colour – calls that would suggest an increased consumer demand – do not necessarily translate into a greater number of Black authors and authors of colour being published, nor an increase in the diversity of subjects and genres that Black authors and authors of colour are afforded the opportunity by publishers to write. Here we can see the rigidity of the logic of White taste and how the assumptions around readers that structure this logic, perhaps unconsciously, take precedence above clear commercial opportunities.

5 Conclusion

In her 2020 essay collection, *Just Us*, Claudia Rankine tells a story about a friendship she developed from an interaction with a White man on an aeroplane. While sitting next to one another on the aeroplane, the conversation turned to race. The man said to Rankine, 'I don't see color' (49), to which Rankine replied, 'Ain't I a Black woman?'. The White man on the aeroplane also spoke of his hometown and the nature of the relationship between the Black and the White children when he was growing up. A short time after the flight, the White man wrote a letter to Rankine, reflecting on the conversation they had about race during their flight. He wrote:

> I told you I didn't notice much tension between the black kids and the white kids in our town … I guess it's not that I didn't notice it so much as I wanted to forget it, because thinking back, the tension was everywhere … I remember only a couple of fights between black kids and white kids, but cruelty, from mostly white to black, was only a comment away. (Rankine 2020, 53)

Writing about this exchange, Rankine (2020, 55) interrogates the 'culture of Whiteness' and privilege of forgetting, writing:

> The lack of an integrated life means that no part of his life recognized the treatment of Black people as an important disturbance … Though my seatmate misrepresented the fact of the matter, he did not misrepresent the role those facts played in his own life. I don't doubt that he believed what he said at the time.

I like to think of this exchange between Rankine and her travel companion as a metaphor for conversations around race and White supremacy that circulate through the contemporary publishing sector. People of colour working in the sector agitate and lobby and advocate for transformation, the White people working in the sector listen and reflect and remain. Like the

White man in Rankine's story, there may be a moment of reflection or even a mea culpa, but with or without this reflection, the benefits of the inequality that plagues the publishing sector flows to White people. The privilege of misremembering falls to White individuals, but it is perpetuated systemically.

Rankine's White seatmate reveals an initial lack of reflection or personal interrogation about the nature of race and White supremacy in his upbringing. When asked about the relationships between the Black and the White children in his hometown, he responds with an unformed and under-examined answer, as evidenced by his subsequent letter. I would argue that the White man's unformed answer is based upon an uncritical assumption about his own experiences, a White solipsism perhaps. If we take the White man's assumption as a single data point among millions, we can see the way that White consensus forms around an assumption that there was no racial tension in anyone's particular hometown. What, then, does this story suggest about assumptions, consensus and White dominance in book culture?

In many ways, the structure of the contemporary Anglophone publishing sector has remained unchanged over the past 200 years. Despite near-constant technological upheaval and corporate evolution, in many ways the publishing sector and the radiating book culture appear resistant to change and transformation. In the United States, the United Kingdom and Australia, the leaders in the sector – the publishers, the editors, the canonical authors – are and have always been White. And so, the racist assumptions around authority, legitimacy and class that underpin the conceptions of an 'author' in the eighteenth century remain unchallenged and become baked into the fabric of the industry with every new White publisher, every new White commissioning editor, every new White literary celebrity. Like Rankine's White seatmate, in the collective imagination of the White-dominant industry, this assumption of White leadership goes unchallenged. The industry evolves into one that is built for White people (Pham 2021).

However, the White-dominant structure of contemporary publishing and the assumptions that underpin this dominance *have* been challenged. There is a long history of authors, critics and scholars calling attention to the deep inequality and inequities that define publishing and book culture (see, for example, hooks 1989; Morrison 1992; Moreton-Robinson 2000; Ramdarshan Bold 2019; Chowdhury 2021), and still transformation of these structures consistently appears beyond reach. The logic of White taste, and the assumptions upon which this logic is structured, is so embedded in the sector that it has become the baseline from which all activities are performed. We can see the logic of White taste in action in the diversity and inclusion statements from major global publishing houses: Penguin Random House's (2021) statement claims that the publisher, 'must give a platform to an even broader range of voices, especially more authors and illustrators of color'; Faber and Faber's (2022) statement says, 'We are working to ensure that voices we have under-represented are heard in all parts of our publishing, across our adult and children's lists'; and, Simon and Schuster's President and CEO, Jonathan Karp (2021) notes that the company 'look to foster and nurture a vibrant and stimulating culture of awareness and inclusion, in order that we may better identify and champion a diverse range of authors and viewpoints'.

These three statements are broadly illustrative of the nature of conversations around diversity and inclusion in contemporary book culture (Saha and van Lente 2022), they reveal not only a lack of real, measurable commitment to any meaningful change, but also a deeply-rooted assumption about who currently maintain, and who will continue to maintain, power in the sector. All these statements assume that the decision-makers are White and that they will afford greater access to Black authors and authors of colour. Equality, in these instances, is determined by the size of the platform for authors of colour that publishers decide to establish. And underpinning the assumption around the nature and profile of power in publishing houses, exists the assumption that White authors are legitimate authors and Black authors and authors of colour must be afforded the opportunity to write, to be authors, on the terms set out by White publishers. Rather than address the inequity that defines the sector, these statements contribute to its continuation.

The solution to this inequality will not come about with corporate statements about diversity and inclusion, or White women's prizes, or anti-racist reading lists. The solution to this inequality can be found in breaking the logic that defines publishing practice. I do not know what that looks like, but I believe it begins with bringing this logic into the light.

References

Adler, M. and Harper, L. M. (2018). Race and Ethnicity in Classification Systems: Teaching Knowledge Organization from a Social Justice Perspective. *Library Trends* 67 (1), 52–73.

Ahmed, S. (2012). *On Being Included: Racism and Diversity in Institutional Life*. Chapel Hill: Duke University Press.

Allington, P. (2011). What is Australia Anyway? The Glorious Limitations of the Miles Franklin Literary Award. *Australian Book Review*.

Anand, N. and Jones, B. C. (2008). Tournament Rituals, Category Dynamics, and Field Configuration: The Case of the Booker Prize. *Journal of Management Studies* 45 (6), 1036–60.

Anderson, P. (2020). US Publishers, Authors, Booksellers Call Out Amazon's 'Concentrated Power' in the Market. *Publishing Perspectives*, 17 August. https://publishingperspectives.com/2020/08/us-publishers-authors-book sellers-call-out-amazons-concentrated-power-in-the-book-market/ (accessed 17 June 2022).

Angelou, M. (1969). *I Know Why the Caged Bird Sings*. New York: Random House.

APA Style (2022). Racial and Ethnic Identity. *American Psychological Association*. https://apastyle.apa.org/style-grammar-guidelines/bias-free-language/racial-ethnic-minorities(accessed 17 June 2022).

Appiah, A. K. (2020). The Case for Capitalising the *B* in Black. *The Atlantic*, 18 June. www.theatlantic.com/ideas/archive/2020/06/time-to-capitalize-blackand-white/613159/ (accessed 17 June 2022).

Baldwin, J. (1955). *Notes of a Native Son*. Boston: Beacon Press.

Bourdieu, P. (1977). *Outline of a Theory of Practice*. Cambridge: Cambridge University Press.

Bourdieu, P. (1984). *Distinction: A Social Critique of the Judgement of Taste*. Cambridge: Harvard University Press.

Bourdieu, P. (1993). *The Field of Cultural Production: Essays on Art and Literature*. New York: Columbia University Press.

Butterfield, S. (1974). *Black Autobiography in America*. Amherst: University of Massachusetts Press.

Caro, J. (2015). Why the Bias against Female Authors? *Sydney Morning Herald*, 19 August. www.smh.com.au/opinion/we-havent-come-that-far-since-19th-century-women-writers-used-male-pen-names-20150818-gj1jf6.html (accessed 19 December 2022).

Cattani, G., Ferriani, S. and Allison, P. D. (2014). Insiders, Outsiders, and the Struggle for Consecration in Cultural Fields: A Core-Periphery Perspective. *American Sociological Review* 79 (2), 258–81.

Childress, C., Rawlings, C. M. and Moeran, B. (2017). Publishers, Authors, and Texts: The Process of Cultural Consecration in Prize Evaluation. *Poetics* 60, 48–61.

Chowdhury, R. (2021). It's Hard to Be What You Can't See: Diversity within Australian Publishing. *2019–2020 Beatrice Davis Editorial Fellowship Report*. www.publishers.asn.au/common/Uploaded%20files/APA%20Resources/Research/BDEF/BDEF%202019-2020%20Report%20-%20Radhiah%20Chowdhury.pdf (accessed 19 December 2022)

Clement, M., Proppe, D. and Rott, A. (2007). Do Critics Make Bestsellers? Opinion Leaders and the Success of Books. *Journal of Media Economics* 20(2), 77–105.

Cooter, M. (1987). *Reviewing the Reviews: A Woman's Place on the Page*. Ann Arbor: University of Michigan Press.

Crenshaw, K. (1989). Demarginalizing the Intersection of Sex and Race: A Black Feminist Critique of Antidiscrimination Doctrine. *University of Chicago Legal Forum* 1 (8). www.australianbookreview.com.au/abr-online/archive/2011/55-june-2011/395-what-is-australia-anyway (accessed 12 January 2022).

Cunningham, S. (2011). A Prize of One's Own: Flares, Cock-Forests and Dreams of a Common Language. *Kill Your Darlings*, 1 October. www .killyourdarlings.com.au/article/a-prize-of-ones-own-flares-cock-forests-and-dreams-of-a-common-language/ (accessed 19 December 2022).

Dane, A. (2020a). Cultural Capital as Performance: Tote Bags and Contemporary Literary Festivals. *Memoires du Livre/Studies in Book Culture* 11 (2), 1–30.

Dane, A. (2020b). Eligibility, Access and the Laws of Literary Prizes. *Australian Humanities Review* 66 (May), 122–36.

Dane, A. (2020c). *Gender and Prestige in Literature: Contemporary Australian Book Culture*. London: Palgrave Macmillan.

Decety, J. (2014). The Complex Relation between Morality and Empathy. *Trends in Cognitive Sciences* 18 (7), 337–9.

DiAngelo, R. (2018). *White Fragility*. Boston: Beacon Press.

Doll, J. (2012). The Ongoing Problem of Race in Y.A. *The Atlantic*, 27 April. www.theatlantic.com/culture/archive/2012/04/ongoing-problem-race-y/328841/ (accessed 17 June 2022).

Driscoll, B. (2014). *New Literary Middlebrow: Reading and Tastemaking in the Twentyfirst Century*. London: Palgrave Macmillan.

DuBois, W. E. B. (1935). *Black Reconstruction in Americaa, 1860–1880*. New York: Harcourt Brace.

Eddo-Lodge, R. (2017). *Why I'm No Longer Talking to White People About Race*. London: Bloomsbury.

English, J. (2005). *The Economy of Prestige: Prizes, Awards, and the Circulation of Cultural Value*. Cambridge: Harvard University Press.

Faber (2020). In Solidarity with the #BlackLivesMatterMovement …. *Tweet Thread*, 3 June. https://twitter.com/FaberBooks/status/1267828761258409990 (accessed 17 June 2022).

Faber (2021). Diversity & Inclusion. www.faber.co.uk/about-faber/social-responsibility/diversity-inclusion/ (accessed 20 June 2022).

Faber and Faber (2022). Diversity Action Plan. www.faber.co.uk/diversity-action-plan/. accessed 12 January 2022.

Foucault, M. (1969). What is an Author? *Lecture for Société Française de Philosophie*, 22 February. www.open.edu/openlearn/pluginfile.php/624849/mod_resource/content/1/a840_1_michel_foucault.pdf (accessed 19 December 2022).

George, G. J. and Leidner, D. E. (2019). From Clicktivism to Hacktivism: Understanding Digital Activism. *Information and Organisation* 22, 1–45.

Glaister, D. (1997). Outsider Scoops Award for Women Writers. *The Guardian*, 5 June.

Gray, H. (2016). Precarious Diversity: Representation and Demography. In M. Curtin and K. Sanson (eds.) *Precarious Creativity: Global Media, Local Labor*. Berkeley: University of California Press, 241–53.

Groves, N. (2015). Emily Bitto Wins 2015 Stella Prize for Her Debut Novel *The Strays*. *The Guardian*, 21 April. www.theguardian.com/books/2015/apr/21/emily-bitto-wins-2015-stella-prize-the-strays (accessed 19 December 2022).

Hachette (2021). Changing the Story. www.hachette.co.uk/landing-page/hachette/changing-the-story/ (accessed 17 June 2022).

Harvey, M. and Lamond, J. (2016). Taking the Measure of Gender Disparity in Australian Book Reviewing as a Field, 1985 and 2013. *Australian Humanities Review* . www.australianhumanitiesreview.org/2016/11/15/taking-the-measure-of-gender-disparity-in-australian-book-reviewing-as-a-field-1985-and-2013/ (accessed 19 December 2022).

Helgason, J., Kaarholm, S. and Steiner, A. (2014). Introduction. In J. Helgason, S. Kaarholm and A. Steiner (eds.) *Hype: Bestsellers in Literary Culture*. Lund: Nordic Academic Press, 7–41.

Hesmondhalgh, D. and Saha, A. (2013). Race, Ethnicity and Cultural Production. *Popular Communications* 11, 179–95.

Hill Collins, P. (2019). *Intersectionality*. Chapel Hill: Duke University Press.

Hogan, K. (2016). *The Feminist Bookstore Movement: Lesbian Antiracism and Feminist Accountability*. Durham: Duke University Press.

hooks, b. (1989). *Thinking Feminist, Thinking Black*. Boston: South End Press.

hooks, b. (2012). *Writing Beyond Race: Living Theory and Practice*. Oxford: Routledge.

Jackson, L. M. (2020). What is an Anti-Racist Reading List For? *Vulture*, 4 June. www.vulture.com/2020/06/anti-racist-reading-lists-what-are-they-for.html (accessed 18 June 2022).

Johnson, A. (1996). Only Women Need Apply for the Richest Literary Prize. *The Guardian*, 26 January.

Karp, J. (2021). Social Impact. Simon & Schuster. www.simonandschuster .com.au/p/social-impact (accessed 20 June 2022).

Kendi, I. X. (2019). *How to Be an Antiracist*. New York: One World.

Kon-Yu, N. (2016). Diversity, the Stella Count and the Whiteness of Australian Publishing. *The Conversation*, 13 December. https://thecon versation.com/diversity-the-stella-count-and-the-whiteness-of-australian-publishing-69976 (accessed 18 June 2022).

Lamond, J. (2011). Stella vs Miles: Women Writers and Literary Value in Australia. *Meanjin*, Spring. https://meanjin.com.au/essays/stella-vs-miles-women-writers-and-literary-value-in-australia/ (accessed 17 June 2022).

Landy, J. (2012). *How to Do things with Fictions*. Oxford: Oxford University Press.

Linden, G., Smith, B. and York, J. (2003). Amazon.com Recommendations: Item-to-Item Collaborative Fitering. *IEE Computer Society*, February. https://cseweb.ucsd.edu//classes/fa17/cse291-b/reading/Amazon-Recommendations.pdf (accessed 17 June 2022).

Lister, D. (1999). Tale of Woe for British Novelists Snubbed for Fiction Prize. *The Independent*, 27 April.

Locke, K. (2017). White Voices: The Dominance of White Authors in Canadian Literary Awards. *The Structure of the Book Publishing Industry in Canada* 371 (Fall), 1–9.

Lorde, A. (1984). *Sister Outsider*. Berkeley: Crossing Press.

Macé, M. (2013). Ways of Reading, Modes of Being. *New Literary History* 44 (2), 213–29.

Maunder, S. (2021). Will Black Lives Matter Bring Lasting Change to Australia's Publishing Industry? *SBS News*, 12 September. www.sbs.com.au/news/article/will-black-lives-matter-bring-lasting-change-to-australias-publishing-industry/ng343ddxr (accessed 17 June 2022).

McGrath, L. B. (2019). Comping White. *LA Review of Books*, 21 January. https://lareviewofbooks.org/article/comping-white/ (accessed 8 November 2022).

Miller, L. J. (2000). The Best-Seller List as Marketing Tool and Historical Fiction. *Book History* 3, 286–304.

Moreton-Robinson, A. (2000). *Talkin' Up to the White Woman: Indigenous Women and Feminism*. St Lucia: University of Queensland Press.

Morrison, T. (1992). *Playing in the Dark: Whiteness and the Literary Imagination*. Cambridge: Harvard University Press.

Mosse, K. (1996). When Words Fail – Kate Mosse, Chair of the Orange Prize Argues that Fellow Judges' Reported Criticisms of the Quality of Entrants to the £30,000 Women-Only Fiction Award Have Been Misrepresented. *The Guardian*, 16 April.

National Association of Black Journalists (2020). NABJ Statement on Capitalizing Black and Other Racial Identifiers. www.nabj.org/page/styleguide (accessed 17 June 2022).

Nayak, A. (2007). Critical Whiteness Studies. *Sociology Compass* 12 (1), 737–55.

New York Times (2022a). Bestsellers Methodology. www.nytimes.com/books/best-sellers/methodology/ (accessed 17 June 2022).

New York Times (2022b). Hardback Non-Fiction Bestsellers, 3 May–27 July 2020. www.nytimes.com/books/best-sellers/hardcover-nonfiction/ (accessed 16 November 2022).

New York Times (2022c). Hardback Non-Fiction Bestsellers, 2 May–25 July 2021. www.nytimes.com/books/best-sellers/hardcover-nonfiction/ (accessed 16 November 2022).

New York Times (2022d). Hardback Fiction Bestsellers, 2 May–25 July 2021. www.nytimes.com/books/best-sellers/hardcover-fiction/ (accessed 16 November 2022).

Noble, S. U. (2018). *Algorithms of Oppression: How Search Engines Reinforce Racism*. New York: New York University Press.

Norris, S. (2006). The Booker Prize: A Bourdieusian Perspective. *Journal for Cultural Research* 10 (2), 139–58.

Olney, J. (1980). Autobiography and the Cultural Moment: A Thematic, Historical, and Bibliographical Introduction. In J. Olney (ed.) *Autobiography*. Princeton: Princeton University Press, 3–27.

Olson, H. A. (2007). How We Construct Subjects: A Feminist Analysis. *Library Trends* 56 (2), 509–41.

Orange Prize for Fiction (2003). https://web.archive.org/web/20030425050348/http://195.157.68.238/faqs/howsetup.html (accessed 19 December 2022).

Ortega, M. (2006). Being Lovingly, Knowingly Ignorant: White Feminism and Women of Colour. *Hypatia* 21 (3), 56–74.

Painter, N. I. (2020). Why 'White' Should Be Capitalized, Too. *The Washington Post*, 22 July. www.washingtonpost.com/opinions/2020/07/22/why-white-should-be-capitalized/ (accessed 17 June 2022).

Parnell, C. (2022). *Platform Publishing in the Entertainment Ecosystem: Experiences of Marginalised Authors on Amazon and Wattpad.* PhD Thesis, University of Melbourne.

Penguin Random House (2021). Diversity, Equity & Inclusion. https://social-impact.penguinrandomhouse.com/our-commitments/diversity-equity-inclusion/ (accessed 17 June 2022).

Pham, C. (2021). Interview #174: Radhiah Chowdhury. *Liminal*, 10 May. www.liminalmag.com/interviews/radhiah-chowdhury (accessed 17 June 2022).

Pouly, M.-P. (2016). Playing Both Sides of the Field: The Anatomy of a 'Quality' Bestseller. *Poetics* 59, 20–34.

Pressman, J. (2020). *Bookishness: Loving Books in a Digital Age.* New York: Columbia University Press.

Pruett, J. (2022). NYT Hardcover Fiction Bestsellers. *Post45 Collective.* https://doi.org/10.18737/CNJV1733p4520220211 (accessed 20 June 2022).

Publishers Association (2020). Diversity Survey of the Publishing Workforce 2020. www.publishers.org.uk/publications/diversity-survey-of-the-publishing-workforce-2020/ (accessed 17 June 2022).

Ramdarshan Bold, M. (2019). *Inclusive Young Adult Fiction: Authors of Colour in the United Kingdom.* London: Palgrave Macmillan.

Rankine, C. (2020). *Just Us: An American Conversation.* Minneapolis: Graywolf Press.

Reid, C. (2020). Diversity in Publishing in the Ages of Black Lives Matter. *Publishers Weekly*, 14 August. www.publishersweekly.com/pw/by-topic/industry-news/publisher-news/article/84107-diversity-in-publishing-in-the-age-of-black-lives-matter.html (accessed 17 June 2022).

Saad, L. F. (2020). Do the Work: An Anti-Racist Reading List. *The Guardian*, 2 June. www.theguardian.com/books/booksblog/2020/jun/03/do-the-work-an-anti-racist-reading-list-layla-f-saad (accessed 18 June 2022).

Saha, A. (2016). Rationalizing/Racializing Logic of Capital in Cultural Production. *Media Industries Journal* 3(1), 1–13.

Saha, A. and van Lente, S. (2020). Re-thinking 'Diversity' in Publishing. *Report for Spread the Word, Arts and Humanities Research Council and Goldsmiths University*. www.spreadtheword.org.uk/wp-content/uploads/2020/06/Rethinking_diversity_in-publishing_WEB.pdf (accessed 17 June 2022).

Saha, A. and van Lente, S. (2022). The Limits of Diversity: How Publishing Industries Make Race. *International Journal of Communication* 16, 1804–22.

Smith, J. (1996). And the Winner is . . . A Woman? It is Open to More Writers Than Any Other Literary Award in the World, So What's the Problem. *The Guardian*, 26 January.

So, R. J. (2021). *Redlining Culture: A Data History of Racial Inequality and Postwar Fiction*. New York: Columbia University Press.

Squires, C. (2013). Literary Prizes and Awards. In G. Harper (ed.) *A Companion to Creative Writing*. Chichester: John Wiley, 291–303.

Squires, C. (2017). Taste or Big Data? Post-Digital Editorial Selection. *Critical Quarterly* 59 (3), 24–38.

Steger, J. (2013). Stella Longlist Ranges Far and Wide. *The Age*, 21 February. www.theage.com.au/entertainment/books/stella-prize-longlist-ranges-far-and-wide-20130221-2et1w.html (accessed 19 December 2022).

Steiner, A. (2014). Serendipity, Promotion, and Literature: The Contemporary Book Trade and International Megasellers. In J. Helgason, S. Kaarholm and A. Steiner (eds.) *Hype: Bestsellers in Literary Culture*. Lund: Nordic Academic Press, 55–90.

Stella Prize (2019). Judges Report. https://thestellaprize.com.au/prize/2019-prize/ (accessed 17 June 2022).

Stella Prize (2021). About the Prize. https://thestellaprize.com.au/prize/about-the-prize/ (accessed 17 June 2022).

Steyn, M. and Conway, D. (2010). Intersecting Whiteness, Interdisciplinary Debates. *Ethnicities* 10 (3), 283–91.

Sullivan, J. (2012). A Women's Place. *Sydney Morning Herald*, 13 January. smh.com.au/entertainment/books/a-womans-place-20120113-1pyoa .html (accessed 19 December 2022).

Sutherland, J. (2007). *Bestsellers: A Very Short Introduction*. Oxford: Oxford University Press.

Travis, T. (2008). Women in Print Movement: History and Implications. *Book History* 11, 275–300.

Twine, F. W. and Gallagher, C. (2008). The Future of Whiteness: A Map of the 'Third Wave'. *Ethnic and Racial Studies* 31 (1), 4–24.

van Rees, C. R. (1987). How Reviewers Reach Consensus on the Value of Literary Works. *Poetics* 16, 275–94.

Verso Books (2020). Today, June 8 2020, Workers in Publishing & Media …. *Tweet Thread*, 8 June. https://twitter.com/VersoBooks/ status/1269932182426001412?ref_src=twsrc%5Etfw%7Ctwcamp% 5Etweetembed%7Ctwterm%5E1269932700472954880%7Ctwgr%5E% 7Ctwcon%5Es2_&ref_url=https%3A%2F%2Fpublishingperspectives. com%2F2020%2F06%2Fus-publishing-day-of-action-calls-indsutry- racial-disparities-into-question%2F (accessed 17 June 2022).

Vezzali, L., Stathi, S., Giovannini, D., Capozza, D. and Trifiletti, E. (2014). The Greatest Magic of Harry Potter: Reducing Prejudice. *Journal of Applied Psychology* 45 (2), 105–21.

Viltus, S. (2020). How the Black Lives Matter Protests Impacted Book Media. *Book Riot*, 11 September. https://bookriot.com/black-lives-matter- in-book-media/ (accessed 17 June 2022).

Wallace, D. (2018). Cultural Capital as Whiteness? Examining Logics of Ethno-Racial Representation and Resistance. *British Journal of Sociology of Education* 39 (4), 466–82.

Weber, M. (2018). *Literary Festivals and Contemporary Book Culture*. London: Palgrave Macmillan.

Women's Prize for Fiction (2021). Our Story. www.womensprizeforfiction
.co.uk/our-story (accessed 17 June 2022).

Wyndham, S. (2013). Stellar Shortlist for New Women's Book Prize.
Sydney Morning Herald, 20 March.

Zangen, B. (2003). Women as Readers, Writers and Judges: The
Controversy about the Orange Prize for Fiction. *Women's Studies* 32
(3), 281–99.

Cambridge Elements ≡

Publishing and Book Culture

SERIES EDITOR
Samantha Rayner
University College London

Samantha Rayner is Professor of Publishing and Book Cultures at UCL. She is also Director of UCL's Centre for Publishing, co-Director of the Bloomsbury CHAPTER (Communication History, Authorship, Publishing, Textual Editing and Reading) and co-Chair of the Bookselling Research Network.

ASSOCIATE EDITOR
Leah Tether
University of Bristol

Leah Tether is Professor of Medieval Literature and Publishing at the University of Bristol. With an academic background in medieval French and English literature and a professional background in trade publishing, Leah has combined her expertise and developed an international research profile in book and publishing history from manuscript to digital.

About the series

This series aims to fill the demand for easily accessible, quality texts available for teaching and research in the diverse and dynamic fields of Publishing and Book Culture. Rigorously researched and peer-reviewed Elements will be published under themes, or 'Gatherings'. These Elements should be the first check point for researchers or students working on that area of publishing and book trade history and practice: we hope that, situated so logically at Cambridge University Press, where academic publishing in the UK began, it will develop to create an unrivalled space where these histories and practices can be investigated and preserved.

Cambridge Elements ≡

Publishing and Book Culture

Bestsellers

Gathering Editor: Beth Driscoll

Beth Driscoll is Associate Professor in Publishing and Communications at the University of Melbourne. She is the author of The New Literary Middlebrow (Palgrave Macmillan, 2014), and her research interests include contemporary reading and publishing, genre fiction and post-digital literary culture.

Gathering Editor: Lisa Fletcher

Lisa Fletcher is Professor of English at the University of Tasmania. Her books include Historical Romance Fiction: Heterosexuality and Performativity (Ashgate, 2008) and Popular Fiction and Spatiality: Reading Genre Settings (Palgrave Macmillan, 2016).

Gathering Editor: Kim Wilkins

Kim Wilkins is Professor of Writing and Deputy Associate Dean (Research) at the University of Queensland. She is also the author of more than thirty popular fiction novels.

ELEMENTS IN THE GATHERING

Printed in the United States
by Baker & Taylor Publisher Services